THEATERCRAFT
Creativity & the art of drama

THEATERCRAFT

creativity
& the art
of drama

Nigel Forde

Harold Shaw Publishers
Wheaton, Illinois

The Wheaton Literary Series

Copyright © Nigel Forde, 1986, British edition; 1990, American edition

This edition issued by special arrangement with Monarch Publications, KT House, 1 St. Anne's Road, Eastbourne, East Sussex BN21 3UN, England. Original title: *Theatrecraft: An Actor's Notes on His Trade.*

Cover photo © 1990, Michael Stauffer

ISBN 0-87788-807-8

Library of Congress Cataloging-in-Publication Data
Forde, Nigel.
   [Theatrecraft, an actor's notes on his trade]
   Theatercraft, creativity & the art of drama / Nigel Forde.
     p.   cm. — (The Wheaton literary series)
   Originally published under the title: Theatrecraft, an actor's notes on his trade.
   Bibliography: p.
   Includes index.
   ISBN 0-87788-807-8
   1. Drama in Christian education. 2. Christian drama—Presentation, etc. I. Title. II. Title: Theatercraft, creativity and the art of drama. III. Series.
BV1534.4.F67 1990
246'.7—dc20   89-35361
                                   CIP

---

99 98 97 96 95 94 93 92 91 90

10 9 8 7 6 5 4 3 2 1

Contents

Introduction

*I*f C.S. Lewis had not already used the title, this book might well have been called *They Asked for a Paper*, because it is in response to requests, pleas, even indignant demands, from Christians all around the world, that this book has been written.

What is it? It is a handy guide, an outline, an introduction for Christians to all the different disciplines that are involved in the art of theater. It is a *Vade Mecum*, a kind of equivalent to the engineer's Workshop Manual.

What isn't it? The Alpha and Omega, the Final Word, the Definitive Answer to All Problems that Christians Are Likely to Experience. Nor is it a magic word that can transform a ragged, lazy, uninterested band of self-seeking individuals into a company that will rival the Royal Shakespeare Company. It is not easy.

There are in existence scores of books dealing with different aspects of the theater. I see this one not as an addition to them but as an introduction. If I have any claim at all to be an expert, it is only through experience and reading, both of which I have tried to distill here. Many books could be—and have been—written, by wiser men and women than I, on subjects to which I have devoted only a chapter or so. The serious reader will want to flesh this out by further research and by practical application.

It seemed important, also, that there should be a reference book of this kind written for Christians by a Christian who has been through and can understand many of the problems—theological, moral, practical—that local church drama groups come up against. It is for this reason that I have included material not strictly necessary in a practical manual, but important, I believe, if we are to understand what we are doing, why we are doing it, and what we are up against. We must always be ready to answer questions about the implications of our work on our faith and vice versa. So I have included material about the theology of theater, the distinctive problems of the Christian artist, Christianity and taste, and so on. Thus, while this is not at all a book designed for professionals—as far as practice is concerned—there may be parts which would give the professional pause and help him to see some old questions in a new light. I hope so.

In order not to be accused of sexism, I must also explain that it is for considerations of style alone that I have referred to "the actor" and not "the actor or actress," to "him" rather than "to him and her" throughout the book. To have done otherwise would have been unbearably pedantic and hideously inelegant. As in most English prose, the male embraces the female unless referring to a specific writer or actor.

I have no wish to force any particular method of reading on those who buy this book. My own method is very simple: I start at the beginning and read on through the chapters in numerical order until I get to the end and then I stop, for a while at least. This is the method I recommend for this book. It may be tempting for those who aspire to—or, more likely, have been thrust into—directorial skills to read only the chapter about directing, just as actors may wish to limit themselves to the chapters specifically concerned with stagecraft and acting skills. I won't quarrel with you if you want to start on the chapters dealing with your own, personal hobbyhorse;

but I do want to plead with you to read the other chapters as well, not just in order to get your money's worth, but because theater, like orchestral music, is not dependent on one particular skill exercised in a vacuum. A writer cannot do without actors, the actors cannot do without a director, and a director without actors or writers is a fairly lonely figure.

It is of immense help if each understands the kind of problems faced by the others. An actor will play a scene more intelligently if he knows what the writer was aiming at; the writer will benefit from knowing how actors solve their problems of characterization; the director, like the conductor, needs to know just as much as he can.

Finally, those who know of my long-standing connection with Riding Lights Theatre Company must not assume that ideas and opinions expressed here are identifiable with company policy or thought. Some, I know, are shared by the directorship of Riding Lights; others may not be. I alone must take responsibility for the contents of this book and for all its shortcomings.

Nigel Forde
York, England

Frontispiece

*S*orry. Apparently it is too late for a frontispiece once you've got past the Introduction. If you really need one you could probably draw your own on the inside of the front cover and color it in.

Meanwhile, here is a kind of verbal frontispiece. The book is dedicated to all those pictured within.

One:	Friday night.
Two:	Seven-thirty.
One:	Church Annex.
Two:	"Drama Group."
One:	The first one to arrive
Two:	Is called Terry.
One:	It's funny how the first one to arrive
Two:	Is always called Terry.
One:	He wears a floppy kind of sweater,
Two:	Baggy brown corduroys,
One:	Bright-colored socks,
Two:	Open-toed sandals,
One:	You know the sort of thing—
Two:	Drama Group Clothes.

One: Friday night.

Two: Seven-forty-five.

One: Church Annex.

Two: Still just Terry.

One: Then, breathlessly—hurrying, laughing,

Two: Pushing, joking,

One: Giggling, scrambling

Two: Come

One: The others.

Two: Well . . . some of them.

One: Myra,

Two: Bill,

One: David,

Two: John,

One: Sheila,

Two: Leslie,

One: And—ohhh, you know! . . . the little one with a lisp and brown ski-pants.

Two: And, of course, there's Mrs. Birchfield;

One: There's always Mrs. Birchfield.

Two: Myra says,

One: Hello everyone!

Two: Bill says,

One: Cheers!

Two: David says,

One: Hi, guys!

Two: Mrs. Birchfield says,

One: Bless you!

Two: Terry gets out his green file.

One: Right!

Two: Shouldn't we start with prayer? says Mrs. Birchfield.

One: Oh, er . . . yeah. (Pause) Lord, we just thank you for the privilege . . .

Two:	And then,
One:	Peter arrives.
Two:	Sorry I'm a bit late!
One:	Look Peter,
Two:	Says Terry,
One:	It's five to eight! I mean . . . ! O.K., none of us are perfect . . .
Two:	*Is* perfect: Mrs. Birchfield.
One:	But I think, you know, we ought to ask ourselves just how committed we really are to one another. I mean . . . you arrive late, you hold everything up. We can't do anything, you know, until everyone's here . . .
Two:	Yeah. Sorry.
One:	Yeah. Well. You know . . . (Pause) Lord, we bless you and ask that tonight . . .
Two:	Then Sharon comes in.
One:	Sharon wears a mohair sweater,
Two:	Skin-tight jeans,
One:	Leg-warmers,
Two:	And high heels.
One:	She tosses her blonde hair out of her green eyes.
Two:	Sorry I'm late, Terry.
One:	Oh . . . yeah, well . . . that's all right; we hadn't really started . . .
Two:	Um . . . (Pause) Amen.
One:	Did you see the movie on Channel 4 last night?
Two:	Yeah. It was Clint Eastwood!
One:	Er, come on you guys—we've got to start this sketch. Um . . .
Two:	I don't know if I like them . . .
One:	I like the color. Capezio?
Two:	Yeah, my mom gave me the money.
One:	Well—you can't complain, then!

Two: *Must* make sure the chairs are put back properly tonight.

One: Look, about this sketch—David! Where are you going?

Two: Just be a minute!

One: Anyway, Myra and Sharon, stop talking about shoes.

Two: David comes back from the bathroom,

One: Last night's T.V. is laid to rest,

Two: Terry has silence.

One: Er . . . right . . .

Two: Then the door opens.

One: Oh, hello. Are you guys in here?

Two: We booked it for the Dance Group.

One: Ages ago.

Two: Parish Hall's free.

One: Wendy!

Two: Sharon! Are those new shoes?

One: Friday night.

Two: Twenty-five to nine.

One: Parish Hall.

Two: Drama Group.

One: Come on, look! Sit down.

Two: We've lost thingamajig—you know, the little one with a lisp and brown ski-pants.

One: It's freezing in here!

Two: Can't we go over by the heater?

One: Why don't we do a little warm-up?

Two: Ohhh! What do you want to do a warm-up for?

One: Professionals do.

Two: I don't care if . . . do they? All right, everyone! Warm up!

One: Stand up everyone!

Two: Then the door opens: it is Mrs. Birchfield.

One: She smiles.

Two: Coffee!!

One: Friday night.

Two: Nine o'clock.

One: Parish Hall.

Two: Drama Group.

One: Look, er . . . could we get everybody together, please?

Two: We ought to wash the cups now; they'll get left.

One: I thought we were going to do a warm-up?

Two: Actually, it's called a limber.

One: O.K. then, Tricia can lead the limber.

Two: Tricia? Who's Tricia?

One: You know—the little one with the lisp and the brown ski-pants.

Two: She's gone home.

One: RIGHT!!! We're going to read this sketch!

Two: Quiet everyone!

One: Quiet!

Two: Terry wants us to read this sketch. O.K., Terry.

One: Right. Could you pass my file please?

Two: File?

One: The green one with "DRAMA" on it.

Two: Green file?

One: Yes, it's got "DRAMA" on it in big letters.

Two: There's no file here.

One: Oh, no!

Two: What?

One: I left it in the Church Annex.

Two: I'll go and get it. You do a limber.

One: Friday night.

Two: Nine-twenty-two.

One: Parish Hall.

Two: Drama Group.

One: O.K., now I've only got four copies, so you'll have to share. We need . . . Where's everyone gone?

Two: They had to go home.

One: Home?

Two: We're meant to finish at half-past.

One: My sketch! We never read my sketch!

Two: Terry . . .

One: My sketch . . . !

Two: I'll make you a cup of coffee.

One: My sketch . . . !

Two: We'll both have a cup of coffee. *(From the kitchen)* There's no milk, I'm afraid; only powdered. Don't worry about the sketch. We couldn't have done it anyway—most of them'll be away on the Weekend Retreat.
          (Bang!!!!!!!!)
       Take sugar, Terry? . . . Terry? Terry . . . Terry???

1

The Christian Artist

God must be glad one loves His world so much.
Robert Browning, *Pippa Passes*

*T*here has been much discussion, some of it quite lively, about the position and function of the Christian artist. Before we embark on a book which will examine the techniques and crafts necessary for the practice of one or two of the arts, it is logical first of all to look at what sort of person the artist is and what the process of creativity involves.

One does not often have the chance to hear an artist answer the question "Why do you write (or act or paint)?" Occasionally a writer is asked where he found the material or the inspiration for a certain novel, or an actor is asked how he came to play a particular part, but his role as an artist to start with is assumed. For many Christians, however, a certain suspicion attaches itself to the practicing of an art for its own sake; the interesting question as far as they are concerned might well be, "Why do you do it at all?"

Well, of course, that question could be asked about anything from accounting to plumbing, from fishing to navigating a ship. The reason, I think, that people want to ask it of the artist is that his job does not seem to be particularly useful. There is also, I think, even if only faintly, a hangover from the Puritan attitude to the arts and to the theater in particular: the feeling that they are not very wholesome, that theater people tend to be vain, selfish, egotistical, shallow, arrogant . . . well, you can carry on the list for yourself if you have a thesaurus handy and nothing else to do.

If the critic is being honest and talking from an absolute standard of virtue, then one can reply with honesty that, yes, there probably is just as much of that sort of thing in the theater as there is in the local church congregation, or the camera club, or the flower-arranging classes, or the neighborhood soccer team. For, on the whole, and mixed in with a great deal of virtue as well, that is what human beings are like.

What exactly an artist does and why he does it is a much more interesting question.

The Role of the Artist

One of the marks of the late twentieth century is that it seems to have become the age of corporate and bureaucratic stupidity and sin. I am not suggesting that corporate sin is a purely modern phenomenon, but that it is abroad in the twentieth century in a way that has never been more than hinted at by even the worst of earlier institutions. For the moment, at least, we seem to be done with the Macchiavellis and Hitlers and Borgias, and we are ankle-deep in a nasty little swamp of sin where no individual can be held responsible for anything except by a kind of moral synecdoche, and where it is possible for us to shrug our shoulders despairingly and say, with some justification in the face of the starving in Ethiopia, in the face of Chernobyl, the possibility of Star Wars, the new interest in the arms race, and the imprisonment of people for their faith or for daring to think and speak the truth, "What can I do? That's the way it is under this system. What I think makes no difference; I have no power to change things."

And yet it is just here that the influence of the creative artist on the human soul, the human will, the human outlook, is incalculably great, either for good or ill. He is the one who *can* say something and be heeded. Art and entertainment have always spoken louder than politics.

Shelley may have been indulging in a little wishful thinking when he made his famous statement, "Poets are the unacknowledged legislators of the world," but there is a good deal more truth in that than many critics are willing to allow.

So what is the artist's function? Sometimes he is a kind of court jester to the whole of society: he sees the truth and he speaks it, however uncomfortable it may be. Sometimes the world screams back at him, and sometimes it sits shamefaced and silent. Here is a jester at work in *King Lear*:

Lear:	Dost thou call me fool, boy?
Fool:	All thy other titles thou hast given away; that thou wast born with.
Kent:	This is not altogether Fool, my Lord.
Fool:	No, faith, lords and great men will not let me; if I had a monopoly out, they would have part on't: and ladies too, they will not let me have all the fool to myself; they'll be snatching . . .

* * *

Fool:	Canst tell how an oyster makes his shell?
Lear:	No.
Fool:	Nor I neither, but I can tell why a snail has a house.
Lear:	Why?
Fool:	Why, to put's head in; not to give it away to his daughters, and leave his horns without a case.

And later, one of the Fool's most trenchant remarks to Lear sitting in the stocks:

> *Lear:*   Where learn'd you this, Fool?
> *Fool:*   Not i' the stocks, Fool.

To play the Fool, in this sense, has always been one of the artist's main functions.

Sometimes the artist is a doctor to the world, pointing out diseases, making a prognosis—a line that runs from Bunyan to Solzhenitsyn. Sometimes he is a guide and philosopher, taking you on strange and beautiful journeys to places you would never have found on your own. Sometimes he is a clown and can show you reasons for laughter and delight. Sometimes he is a teacher— though never without one of the other qualities as well—and sometimes even a healer.

Not long after I first became an actor, I went into a school with a theater company to perform a play for children. In the audience was a seven-year-old Asian girl who had been at the school for almost three years and in all that time had not spoken a single word either to her teachers or her classmates. The experience of a play—a simple, almost archetypal fairy tale, *not* a social document—un-locked something in her mind through her imagination and from that day she became a perfectly normal, responsive, interested child.

The Importance of Art

If we are still tempted to think that art is not really important but merely something of a frill, an hour's pleasant pastime but no more, let us look for a moment at how the arts are considered in the communist countries.

There they really believe and act upon what we so often say—that the pen is mightier than the sword; that the good or the harm that can be done to a man's sensibilities far outweighs that which can be done to his physical body. They believe that art is of immense importance, that it affects people's behavior, and, although they might not care to acknowledge the source of the idea, that man does not live by bread alone. If that were not the case, do you think they would bother to ban, exile, or imprison dissident writers? Would they send agents abroad with touring theater companies—as they do—to keep an eye on what was being said and done? Would they make such a fuss about something that was only a harmless, fringe activity and gratuitous to the real business of living? Of course not. They see quite clearly that literature has a profound and ineradicable effect on humanity, that it can affect behavior to such an extent that something has got to be done about it.

I do not want to begin by defining art too closely. This is not in order to avoid the issue, but for just the opposite reason. Definitions usually have the effect of turning us into Humpty-Dumptys—we make the word mean what happens to suit us at the time and become embroiled in a particularly elusive form of literary hide-and-seek which, though it may be fascinating in itself, veers predictably away from even a hesitant conclusion. Art is many things, and there are many things that are not art, though they slide in quietly under the umbrella of art in order not to get their make-up washed off. It is hard enough trying to define a table, let alone art and all the additional metaphysical problems that a word such as this throws up. We know well enough what a table is when we see one.

As far as art is concerned, we can isolate certain factual aspects for ourselves, such as for instance, Tchaikovsky's distinctive use of woodwind, Seurat's technique of building up a picture from tiny dots of color, Hopkins' violent treatment of normal syntax, and these factual aspects are what may render it imitable to a certain extent. But art itself is something more than the sum of its analyzable parts. It is a response of our nature to a work which transcends the selectivity of the artist and contains a rumor of something much further beyond.

To the secular man this response will be secular; to the religious man it will, whatever the stimulus, be religious; for we must all respond according to the sympathetic strings which have been placed inside us. What comes out of a work of art depends as much upon the observer or the listener as upon the artist himself. Those who have ears to hear will hear. This is one of the differences between art and craft, the exact delineations of which have been disputed almost as often as the line dividing verse and prose. Craft knows exactly what its end is and can be judged successful or otherwise by how well it has achieved its end. Its techniques and its results are analyzable in objective terms.

Not so with art. Art makes use of craft along the way—the application of paint in the correct thickness and hues, the skill of the actor or the cellist and so on—but art has significance over and above the useful or well-made object. Of course the actor uses his craft to show the hesitancy or the drunkenness or the wit of the character he is portraying; the art comes in the significance of that quality within the framework of the whole character, and in the quality of that character within the framework of the whole play, balanced against the other characters, against the action and the plot. What two people get from a performance of *All's Well That Ends Well* is likely to be far more different than what the same two people get from looking at the most expensive of kitchen units.

Art requires attention, a hearing, if it is to be allowed to work on us as it should: it cannot be used. Oscar Wilde remarked that all art is useless. By that he did not mean "no good" as we might mean today, but rather that it is revelatory as opposed to functional. Its effect is not measurable. Outside a farm in the village where I grew up was the rotting hulk of a truck that had been there for perhaps ten years. It was "useless" to the farmer, but it was paradise to me. I spent many happy hours playing and imagining there.

Fashion and Truth

What the artist needs is an openness to the supernatural and the imaginative faculty, combined with a heightened insight into the daily, the actual, even perhaps the trivial; all of which might further imply that he is what we generally refer to today as open-minded. I do not believe this to be so, although it is true that artists are very, very rarely dogmatists.

A sensible man is only open-minded until he finds something worthwhile to shut it on. And, the more a man is an artist, the more austerely he abides by his own taste and the less he is liable to be influenced. One cannot be true to oneself and one's vision and purpose and yet still be swayed by every passing breeze of fashion.

It is surely the mark of the immature to chafe and change and compromise until his opinions and tastes conform to the latest word in fashionable sophistication, or, by a kind of inverse snobbery, unsophistication. The artist is not interested in whether his opinions are modern or intellectual according to the latest poll; he is not interested in the party line or the latest bandwagon in either church or state. Like the prophets, his strength lies in his individuality, his non-conformity. And non-conformity is not always avant-garde—it is sometimes just the opposite. True art nearly always surprises or shocks, which is why it is not always easily acceptable. But one must not seek to shock for its own sake.

No teacher, according to Renoir, can pass on the secret of what true art is. It is a *certain quelque chose* which one carries inside. Elsewhere it has been defined as the exceptional privilege of preserving into adulthood the poetic innocence which truly belongs to childhood. To the merely clever this must appear as nothing more than foolish. In Christian terms, however, this is not an unfamiliar position to occupy.

Some Christian Problems

To be foolish in the eyes of the world is an occupational hazard for the Christian, and when we come to consider the Christian artist we encounter problems which belong to him alone. The three main ones are the problem of modernity, the problem of excellence, and the problem of subject matter.

There is a kind of distancing which time gives to both art and artists. At its best, such distancing enhances understanding and allows the work to be seen both as an individual entity with its own life, depth, and meaning, and also as part of what we can only call a tradition. At its worst this distancing produces a forced and false reverence or, conversely, a revulsion based on nothing more solid than a mere change in style or taste. This is the problem of modernity.

It is as logically foolish to accept something because it is up-to-date as it is to accept something merely because it is old. To do either is unsafe and lamentably unintelligent. There *must* be something more trustworthy than the clock on which to base artistic judgment. There must, too, be something more trustworthy than individual taste. We do not appreciate the worth or value of something by liking it or disliking it; worth and greatness are not mere matters of taste. We can appreciate a perfectly cooked dish even when we are unable to eat it for constitutional reasons.

Christians seem particularly prone to the disease of needing modernity at all costs, of throwing out everything old and replacing it with the up-to-date. In some respects it is an understandable bias, but it does carry with it the danger of throwing out the baby with the bathwater, or at least of changing one bathful of dirty water for another.

G.K. Chesterton in his essay "On Man: Heir of All the Ages" hits the nail on the head when he says, "Any man who is cut off from the past . . . is a man most unjustly disinherited." And yet, in a world where everything is becoming increasingly throw-away and superficial, where language is getting as thin as tissue-paper for want of proper usage, where pop music and sports reign supreme in all the media, where education is for short-term objectives rather than future self-fulfillment, where the "instant" is preferred to the "gradual," where functionality has replaced beauty, Christians are not only standing back and letting it happen, they are actively participating.

"Relevant" is a word we hear bandied about the churches these days; the worship must be "relevant." And what does that mean? Well, usually not relevant to God, but trite enough not to awaken any fresh impression in man. Very often it means that it is of a wishy-washy, mediocre quality that offends very few and attracts very few—the sort of thing that Mr. Average is used to on television commercials. And is man involved, so that he can be lifted up by the beauty of the music into meditation in the presence of God, given a glimpse of his richness, his glory, and his power? Well, he can clap to the rhythm.

It is unspoken, but understood, that nothing written in, say, 1700 can possibly be relevant to a man living in the twentieth century. The crassness of this kind of reasoning does not need pointing out. It is perhaps worth saying that, on television, the results of trying to be relevant are soap-operas, cop series, and situation comedies. The thoughtful and thought-provoking plays are produced by people trying to be truthful. Yes, there are areas in which the two overlap, but, on the whole, relevance is a way of referring to the process of reducing people to a lowest common denominator.

There is a sense abroad in the churches that anything of real beauty, anything crafted with skill and care, anything that can be called art, particularly if it was written more than fifty years ago, cannot be a fit vehicle for the worship of God. Try telling a friend that you have just bought two new worship tapes and then pass him Handel's *Messiah* and look at the surprise on his face. That's not worship, that's art.

In *One Heart, One Voice*[1] Andrew Maries has written a book full of good things. His advice for running a choir is a paradigm for the running of any group of Christians, and I recommend it as a basis for the drama group. I question neither his spiritual wisdom nor his musicianship, but I am worried by one or two strange statements in an earlier part of the book.

He continually refers to a congregation as an entity whose taste, age, and intellect, he believes, can be discovered. Does this really make sense? Even the dullest church does not consist entirely of fifty-three-year-old businessmen who have had the same education, read the same books and magazines, and share a taste for Mantovani, lasagna, Venetian blinds, and retrievers called Prince.

In the congregation that Andrew Maries serves, you can find a twelve-year-old girl standing next to a man of seventy, a Dire Straits fanatic next to a string-quartet player, a solicitor next to a traffic cop, a Ph.D. next to a bus driver—which is just how it should be. The common denominator has nothing at all to do with taste, age, or intellect, and everything to do with the love of God.

A congregation is made up of quite diverse individuals with individual tastes. It is true that a crowd or a mob can be manipulated by an unscrupulous leader until the individuals are sunk and carried away by a kind of mass-hysteria; but it is wrong and dangerous to suggest that congregations are subject to that kind of leading. People do not come to church and shed their intelligence and taste along with their hats and gloves. This is why no one approach will suit any congregation. As Maries says:

Music needs to scratch where the congregations itches! It has to be functional and relevant to their needs. The best music for

worship will be that which sums up the heart of the people and
with which they can identify most.

I wonder whether this is not just wishful thinking, whether it is not
likely to condemn a congregation to a stolid diet of mediocre music
that is actually not completely to anybody's tastes. Is there, for
instance, no chance of showing the congregation an itch it didn't
even know about? No chance of a delightful surprise? No music
for the sheer delight of music? No, for music is only a means to an
end. Maries goes on to tell how Michael Baughen likened music in
worship to a can-opener. You could buy a gold-plated one; it would
look beautiful to you and you could admire it, even get extra
pleasure out of opening the can. But he goes on to say,

> But you need one of ordinary steel with a sharp point to get at
> the nourishing contents inside. When you have opened it you
> don't sit down and wonder about the beauty of the tin-opener
> (*but think of the extra pleasure you could get if you did*), your focus
> of attention is now on the contents.

What a Puritan kind of worship this is where the end can justify
the means, but the means are, in themselves, worthless. Would you,
we might reply, use a germ-ridden, rusty, dangerous can-opener
picked up in a rubbish dump? Presumably, if function is all, the
answer is *yes*.

I think there is real danger in the sort of argument that says that
the excellent and the beautiful must be avoided simply because
they are excellent and beautiful, and implies that congregations
should not like them anyway. Who are we to tell people what they
like and dislike? What works for them and what doesn't? We are
not patronizing arbiters of taste. I am *not* suggesting that we should
enjoy the gift and ignore the Giver; but why should we reject the

gift? Beautiful gifts reflect the Giver I know better than cheap ones do. If, as I suspect, it is merely a matter of taste, why can we not have *both* and allow everyone to worship? C.S. Lewis seems to be much nearer the mark:

> There are two musical situations on which I think we can be confident that a blessing rests. One is where a priest or an organist, himself a man of trained and delicate taste, humbly and charitably sacrifices his own (aesthetically right) desires and gives the people humbler and coarser fare than he would wish, in a belief (even, as it may be, the erroneous belief) that he can thus bring them to God. The other is where the stupid and unmusical layman humbly and patiently, and above all silently, listens to music which he cannot, or cannot fully, appreciate, in the belief that it somehow glorifies God, and that if it does not edify him this must be his own defect ... But where the opposite situation arises, where the musician is filled with the pride of skill or the virus of emulation and looks with contempt on the unappreciative congregation, or where the unmusical, complacently entrenched in their own ignorance and conservatism, look with the restless and resentful hostility of an inferiority complex on all who would try to improve their taste—there, we may be sure, all that both offer is unblessed and the spirit that moves them is not the Holy Ghost.[2]

The problem of modernity and the problem of excellence have now become very much entwined; I have found it impossible to discuss the first without bringing in the second because I cannot subscribe to the view that what is modern is necessarily good. I have digressed, too, into a discussion of music because the overwhelming desire for modernity is particularly noticeable in this area; but there is a similar unwillingness to benefit from the past in the literary sphere as well.

Great minds have produced great things for the sake of God. To refuse to have anything to do with the product of an intellect whose only fault is to have died is both an intellectual and a spiritual arrogance, and ensures that changes will simply move the church out of one straitjacket into another which, all too often, has not even excellence to recommend it.

Apart from the Bible itself, the earliest writing to be found in the average Christian bookstore is by C.S. Lewis. It is a maverick bookstore indeed that displays St. Augustine or Aquinas, G.K. Chesterton, á Kempis, Donne, Traherne, or Hopkins, though they deal in truths which the modern evangelical seems just to be discovering. Can it be true that, unless a book comes out under a Christian imprint, it cannot be worth reading?

It is a very real problem for the Christian writer (or musician for that matter) if he is going to be attended to only so long as he is a fashionable contemporary. In the worst imaginable cases, in desperation to be heard and understood, he may well be forced to leave issues which he wants to and feels able to deal with, in favor of those he feels people will want to listen to.

More and more, the Christian should be involving himself with the life and culture of the society to which he belongs, without having to compromise what he feels he should be saying, and without having to ignore his Christian faith. To do this requires a great deal of understanding and trust on the part of the church, which has withdrawn itself gradually but unmistakably from the mainstream of artistic movements over the last few centuries. Thus, a vicious circle of sorts has been formed. The church withdraws its support, so art becomes more secular, which in turn forces the church to retreat even further, and so on. The distrust and misunderstanding which has grown up toward the arts in general on the part of Christians must now be replaced by a willingness to appreciate the real validity of art to move the emotions and to explore aspects of truth, to enrich our lives and our imaginations.

This cannot and will not happen if we continue to fill our services with rubbish: with third-rate music of the sort that falls upon our ears from loudspeakers in supermarkets, and with theater which is bland, inept, and simplistic propaganda.

Art and Integrity

I have heard it said, from both pew and pulpit, that there is something suspicious about Christians applying themselves to the attainment of excellence. That I find a hard concept to defend. There are certainly spiritual dangers and some hard questions of motive involved in wanting to be the best, but how can it be true that excellence is the one quality that must be denied to Christians?

The parable of the talents seems to teach that we have a God-given *duty* to make the most of what we are given, and I can find no evidence that it should be interpreted solely on a spiritual plane. Even in a fallen world I would hope that if I were to go to a Christian mechanic to get my car mended, or to a Christian dentist to get my teeth fixed, I could be sure that they would do the very best job they were capable of. I don't make the mistake of believing that *because* they are Christians, they are therefore better or more skilled at their jobs than the atheist down the road, but I *do* expect them to take infinite trouble, to treat me with the utmost consideration, and to be perfectly honest. If they are not the best at their jobs, they ought to be as good as they can be.

I carry the same convictions into the world of the arts: One should not strive to be second-rate. If an actor—or a writer—is second-rate and a Christian, it should be because he is not capable of being first-rate, not that he is not trying to be.

And then there is the issue of pride. Ironically, most of the really capable people I know aren't very proud of themselves; it is the second- and third-rate ones who are really cocky. To be proud of yourself you have to have a fair capacity for self-deception, and that is not part of a real artist's make-up.

Let us not forget, though, that God looked at his creation and saw that it was good. Was God guilty of pride? Not at all. It *was* good, and if God had said that it was not good, then he would have been a liar. It can be the same with our own creations; sometimes we can do something that is good. Why should we not admit it? A mechanic ought to know when he has mended a car, when it is safe, when he has done a good job. And it is his job to know. It is the same with an artist. He ought to know when he has written a good play or given a good performance; if he doesn't know, then he does not understand his art. There is nothing sinful in looking back and saying, "Yes, I got it right tonight; it was good." You can never hope to improve if you never know what is good and what isn't. If you are capable of self-criticism, you must be capable of reasoned self-praise.

There is no greater pride—though it comes out in a twisted and inverted form—than the awful false modesty that will not admit to anything more than mere competence. How rude it is when a member of the audience comes to congratulate you on an impressive performance, which has moved or awakened him in some way, if you reply by denying his judgment and telling him how awful you really were. One must be objective with one's own work as one is objective with that of others: if it is good, admit it, enjoy it, and go on and make it even better.

It is a mistake to believe that there are two different sorts of art: Christian art and everybody else's art. Art is not different in this respect from, say, cooking. Good bread made by a pagan is just as nourishing as good bread made by a Christian. The worth and validity of a piece of art stand separate from the beliefs of its creator. And that is true even when those beliefs are embodied in it. Art is not a matter of content but of form.

This may seem a radical thing to say, and whether form and content can ever really be separable is a philosophical question. At least, it becomes a philosophical question after the event, but there is always a stage before the work is created where the two are distinctly separate: where the idea (the content) exists, but has not yet been given shape (the form). The art lies not in thinking, "I shall paint a picture of a café by moonlight," or, "I shall write a poem about the influence of childhood on talent," or even, "I shall play Othello," but in actually doing so. That is where the work starts, and that is where the artist's real problems lie—in matching form with content. There are two ways in which the content will modify the form and vice-versa, but art is the embodiment of ideas, imaginative experiences, and the transmutation of the world, not the world itself. The world itself is reality.

Sacred and Secular

Now a major problem for the Christian artist is his audience—those who are going to accept or reject his offering. And the problem is that he is liable to fall between two stools. Engraved on the seat of one is the legend "Christian" and on the other "Secular." We have already seen that the artist's response to his environment, to the various stimuli which come his way, will be either secular or religious depending on the artist. The problem is that while he sees that, his audience very often does not. To put it at its lowest possible level, the secular observer will object to the content if there is very much that is redolent of a belief in it, while the Christian is puzzled if he cannot find anything that is reducible to a message. Many are the Christian writers who have had to explain how their work can be Christian when it fails to mention the cross, or God, or salvation, but merely fulfills the aims it set out with.

The simple answer is, of course, that only people can be Christians. The adjective "Christian" is completely meaningless unless it refers to a human being. It would be tempting to think otherwise, but knotty problems follow and further definition is always needed. What, for instance, would one mean by "Christian art"? Is a picture of a blade of grass painted by a Christian, Christian art? Is a sincere and moving *Magnificat* and *Nunc Dimittis* set by an atheist Christian music? Is pottery made by Christians Christian tableware? What is the difference between a Christian garden and a secular one?

No—it's best to be logical and admit that Christians are people who sometimes do and make things that are inspired by their beliefs—they write poetry, go to prayer meetings, give away possessions, visit the sick—and who sometimes do things unconnected with religious belief—they water their flowers, write poetry, cook, or take a mistress. For Christians do not have the monopoly on virtuous actions any more than pagans have the monopoly on immoral ones.

There are few artists who are able, psychologically or financially, to pursue their own inspiration and ignore the brickbats of the over-secular who cannot bear the fact that art should ever be able to say something loudly and clearly, and of the over-spiritual who cannot bear a Christian to write about his response to a woman, or to a forest, or to write good documentaries on so-called secular subjects.

What is contrary to Christianity in art which rejoices in fresh air, the sea, the shape of a beech branch, the color of lichen on an old stone wall, the shadow of birds on a hayfield, the love between a man and a woman? They were all created for our delight; why condemn those who find in them beauty and perhaps more than just an intimation of immortality? Some words of Traherne's are not inappropriate:

You never Enjoy the World aright, till the Sea itself floweth in your Veins, till you are clothed with the Heavens, and Crowned with the Stars . . . Till you are as familiar with the Ways of God

in all Ages as with your Walk and Table: till you are intimately
Acquainted with that Shady Nothing out of which the World
was made; till you delight in God for being Good to all: you
never enjoy the World.[3]

The laws of art are the same for Christian and non-Christian
alike. We can return to our image of the loaf of bread: the criterion
of whether it is good or bad has absolutely nothing to do with the
religious beliefs of the cook. It is merely a matter of whether the
recipe has been followed, with or without touches of originality.
There is good art and bad art. Period.

It is necessary to say this because often people make the mistake
of judging the worth of the finished product by the worth of the
cook. Occasionally Christians are drawn to the conclusion that any
artistic attempt aimed at by Christians succeeds simply on account
of their Christianity. Honest, worthy, virtuous, and likable Mr.
Saunders stands up during a service and does a slightly embarrassed and semi-audible recitation which is considered an artistic
triumph, simply because Mr. Saunders is honest, worthy, virtuous,
and likable.

Spiritually speaking this may be an excellent judgment. He may
have given of his best for the sake of God and at considerable
personal sacrifice, which is never an easy thing to do—but, artistically, the judgment is nonsense. If we think back to the first efforts
our children made at, let us say, helping to clean the house, we
applauded them, rightly and properly for their altruism, helpful-
ness, and excellent intentions; and we encouraged them, too. But
their results were probably not the last or even the first word in
domestic craft. We may praise the intention or the result, but let us
not confuse the two.

It is true of art, as of the rest of life that now we see "through a
glass, darkly." It is perhaps particularly true of art that its meaning
is often obscure, parabolic, and, on many levels, allusive. This, after

all, is the way in which it makes its effects. That is not to say it cannot be understood; rather that it cannot properly be explained.

The Artist and Freedom

There is a great deal of freedom—of one sort—around in the arts today; more than there has ever been. It may seem odd to think of freedom as an issue for the Christian artist in the West. Paradoxically, it is not.

Let's make an analogy.

The liberator comes to the prison door, disposes of the guard, flings open the dungeon, and says to the man sitting on his pallet of straw, "I have opened the doors for you! Now you are free!"

What does the liberator—what do *we*—expect the prisoner to do? Naturally, he expects the man to rush, liberated, from his cell into the world of green grass and blue skies. What he does *not* expect him to do is use his freedom to continue sitting in his dungeon and staring at the walls.

And yet, logically, freedom does not imply a particular course of action: it implies choice. If that prisoner is really free, then he must be allowed to stay where he is if that is what he really wants. So often, the freedoms we win are only fresh disorders in disguise. If someone were to come in now and tell me that the government had awarded me a weekly wage for the rest of my life which would free me from having to write, I would thank him politely and carry on writing; if the Women's Liberation movement frees women from the necessity of being housewives and mothers, it must also free them to remain housewives and mothers if they wish. Otherwise the word "freedom" is being misused.

Much of the so-called freedom in the arts is of this nature. Writers and directors have claimed the freedom to portray nudity and explicit sex on stage; the freedom for the actor or the actress to remain clothed is compromised. The freedom to portray on stage or on film scenes of the utmost savagery and violence results in any work of art which understates such violence being labeled as "cozy" or "complacent" or as "shutting its eyes to reality." Real life is all too often defined as that part of real life that fashion dictates we must deal with, but not necessarily morality, good faith, hope, dignity, optimism, and many other unpopular and unfashionable virtues.

The real freedom of the Christian artist is tested by how far he can resist the outrageous nonsense that fashion parades as artistic integrity and put up with the criticism of "smugness" or "bourgeois reactionary" attitudes. But it will also be tested by how far he can put up with misunderstanding and misinterpretation when he speaks disturbingly to Christians. For true freedom is not a gift of institutions or pressure-groups, it is a gift of the Holy Spirit; he who listens to the Holy Spirit will often find his words unacceptable— as did the prophets—by every section of society.

We hear a lot about the artist dwelling in his ivory tower, that mythological haven far from the busy haunts of men. This is not necessarily a seclusion but an exile; it is not that the artist does not want to live among men, but that men don't want artists among them.

There is no decalogue to guide the Christian artist; that is the whole point. But if one had to choose for him a motto, I suppose one could do worse than "To love, and not to twist the facts."

The Artist and His Vision

There is a unique difficulty that today's writers have to face. Every age has its peculiar problems, but this one, it can be argued, is quite different in quality from any previous ones. Until recently every artist has been able to look at the universe as a constant and upon this earth as eternal, at least in comparison with the transitory nature of his short life upon it. It perfectly sums up Shakespeare's attitude.

So long as men can breathe or eyes can see,
So long lives this, and this gives life to thee.

Every writer, until the early years of this century, has been entitled to think in such a way about his work; but the modern artist has no such assurance. He has very little encouragement to build for eternity since it is quite probable that there will not be one. Among all the other horrors of the nuclear threat, this one perhaps has been given very little prominence, but it must be there, even subconsciously, in the minds of all those who are trying to create something of lasting value. The modern artist, then, is probably tempted more than any of his predecessors to abandon the search for perfection and make do with sketches, cartoons, impromptus, improvisations, experiments.

It should not surprise us: art has always reflected the state of mind of the society in which it was created. That is why we can, with a reasonable amount of accuracy, talk of the Age of Reason, the Age of Enlightenment, and so on.

The temptation is to abandon any kind of thoughtful, traditional art and resort to pranks and simple incompetencies. Standards of performance and criticism are no longer measurable; all drops into a great, wild blur of relativism. We are back to "The Emperor's New Clothes"—we dare not say anything because we cannot be sure of our facts, if there still are such things; nothing is worth anything anymore. We don't want to look old-fashioned, dull of vision, philistine, reactionary, and so, paradoxically, we end up becoming just that. We need the courage of that one small child to stand up and shout at the idiots and the impostors, "You aren't wearing any clothes!" A lot of people will scoff, but if they must, they must.

The Christian does have an eternity to look forward to; what he does here and now is going to have eternal consequences. If, as an artist, he is unwilling to put his pen or his mouth or his paintbrush where his heart is—to coin a phrase—he is committing spiritual and artistic suicide. If truth is not his vision and his goal, whatever the cost; if he is willing to slide into a comfortable—but ultimately comfortless—sophistication on the one hand, or an easy reinforcement of Christian cliché on the other, then he will be lost both here and hereafter.

His vision should be one of life as a comedy—in the classical sense of a play with a happy ending where wrongs are righted and all difficulties are overcome—without shutting his eyes to, or trying to belittle, the grave, desperate, obscene, sometimes incomprehensible problems that stand in the way of that happy ending. He is an optimist with every reason for sorrow; a realist with every reason for hope; a puzzle and a paradox like art itself.

Notes

1. Andrew Maries, *One Heart, One Voice*. London: Hodder and Stoughton, 1986, p. 101.

2. C.S. Lewis, "On Church Music" from *Christian Reflections*. Grand Rapids, Mich.: Eerdmans, 1974.

3. Thomas Traherne, "First Century," 29 and 30 from *Centuries of Meditation*. Oxford Standard Authors, 1966.

2

Acting

Think thou and act.
Dante Gabriel Rossetti, *The Choice, III*

Acting is therefore the lowest of the arts, if it is an art at all.
George Moore, *Mummer-Worship*

*W*hen we walk about our own homes, putting a log on the fire, objecting to mashing the potatoes, recounting a funny incident that happened in the office or, on a slightly less mundane level, discussing the latest novel, remembering an incident from a shared past, or criticizing "60 Minutes," we do so perfectly naturally. Our pauses, inflections, and expressions perfectly match what we are saying and the mood in which we are saying it even to the very subtlest degree. We may be pretending to be an acquaintance speaking sarcastically about someone else and showing our own personal feelings about such gossip on our faces: a hard thing to do when you think about it, but we do it—and we do it quite perfectly. Our gestures are not gauche, we do not wonder what to do with our hands, we are not afraid to pause or to use a gesture or an expression of speech. We simply behave.

The art of acting is to be able to reproduce precisely that kind of casual ease on the stage, at will; and not just as ourselves but as any person of any age and background we like to invent from our imaginations.

And when I use the words "casual ease," I do not mean to imply that all acting should be languid, but that it should be straightforward and unforced. Sometimes we may have to be distraught, sometimes menacing, sometimes embarrassed or gauche; but we must not be seen to *act* these emotions—we must find them and reproduce them in a way that matches not our own personality but the personality of the character we are portraying.

So acting isn't terribly special at all. What a disappointment. All we have to do is the sort of thing we do or have done anyway, but we do it deliberately, willingly, consciously. Perhaps that is what George Moore was thinking of when he called acting the lowest of the arts.

The trouble is, of course, that it isn't as simple as that. Things never are, are they? Certainly we are at home metaphorically when we are at home literally and things come easily. But send us empty-handed into a room containing twenty strangers and see how awkwardly and self-consciously we begin to behave. Make us simply walk down an aisle with five hundred silent faces staring at us and see what tricks our limbs, our hearts, our blood begin to play. We are no longer happy simply being ourselves. Then put us on a stage, and the confusion is compounded even further. We are in the most unnatural place in the world, and we have to be at home there; not only that, but with someone else's mind, habits, attitudes, and vocabulary. Perhaps George Moore was right again—it's not an art at all; it is a form of sophisticated torture.

If we allow ourselves to see acting in that light, then disaster will certainly follow. Our bodies will become locked into awkward and unnatural shapes; our muscles will tense up; we will not gesture but twitch; our vocal chords will tense as well, and we shall produce a shallow, strangulated sound that will set the audience's teeth on edge—but not all of them, for we won't be heard past the fourth row of seats; our limbs will refuse to obey the commands sent by the brain, and we will drop props, spill water, trip over carpets, and bump into furniture; our expressions will convey either terror or blankness. We shall, in short, be about as much use to the play as a broken violin with no strings would be to Yehudi Menuhin.

The analogy of a musical instrument is not a bad one for the actor: he should be as old as is necessary to produce the perfect tone, polished, tuned perfectly, ready to respond not only by virtue of the way he is made but also in accordance with any pressure applied upon him by another player.

The actor must be as assured and confident and free on stage in his new persona as he would be merely behaving at home in his own living room. The problem is to find the way to attain this state.

A psychologist once remarked that, had he not heard a choir perform, he would deduce from the number of mechanical skills that, on paper, a chorister has to perform simultaneously, that singing was a physical and mental impossibility. The singer has to read the music, read the words, watch the conductor, breathe at the correct places, work out the pitch of the note he is to sing, and the relative pitch (at the same time as singing a different note), work out the duration of the note, the tone of the note, the volume of the note (which may change as it is being sung), sing the note properly within the phrase and with the correct rhythm, and listen to the rest of the choir to make final adjustments to pitch and phrasing.

Acting is probably of a similar impossibility, for, although a number of these skills will not be necessary to an actor, he must also add to this list movement, gesture, expression, and any stage business that occurs.

That is why rehearsal is such a long and arduous business. Three weeks' work for "two hours' traffic" on the stage? Well, of course it seems like a lot if you think merely in terms of learning lines and remembering moves, but it is a very short time indeed in which to explore all the inflections, all the meanings, all the possibilities, all the implications which any scene from a well-written play will contain. You have to get to know the character you are playing down to the minutest detail before you can be sure of how he—as opposed to *you*—would react to any given circumstance. You have to get to know all the other characters in the play and understand their relationship to you as deeply as is necessary; sometimes as deeply as you know your own friends and relatives.

Not only that, but you have to look at everything in the context of the whole play as well as just how the scene seems to work best. What may work very well in Scene 2 may, if played that way, make nonsense of Scene 12.

Above all, one must avoid second-hand acting. By "second-hand acting" I mean the sort of acting which has its springs in the admiration of a certain actor whom one has seen, usually playing a bravura role—Archie Rice, Richard III, Peer Gynt, Cyrano de Bergerac—and from which one picks certain mannerisms, techniques, or a piece of clever stage business. But we must never be tempted to glue such felicities onto our own performances; to do so is a bit like attempting a limb-transplant in a garden shed with two aspirins and a trowel. We end up not with a revitalized body but with a corpse and a piece left over.

It *is* tempting to come away from the theater thinking, "Ah! So that is the way to express grief/inner turmoil/nobility/greed/overwhelming joy/mental instability," or whatever else has been particularly impressive. But such thoughts must be avoided. The most that can be said is that that was the way in which that particular actor, with that kind of physique, that amount of vocal flexibility, and that number of years of experience under his belt, playing that particular part in that particular way, with that particular cast, set, and costume, made sense of that particular moment—perhaps even only on that particular night. In other words, although it is isolable as a technique, it is the truth only within that particular context.

Now, this kind of thinking is more useful, for it points us not toward stealing other people's "great moments" and sewing them together like patchwork, but toward a method of creativity.

To talk about creativity in terms of method may seem like a paradox, but (paradoxically) it is not. In mathematics, for instance, one does not learn that 12+12=24 and that 457+60=517; one learns a method of addition that will apply to all numbers. This makes it possible to calculate an answer from any given numbers. Mathematical laws seem so set, so logical, so obvious to us today that it is easy to forget that someone, at some time, must have had a hunch that if you were to break down that 457, or that 60, or both of them, into smaller parts, you could *still* get 517 if you added them *all* together. Such a method can be applied to acting.

Now before you lose your eyebrows in your toupee or drop this book into the food processor, consider this for a moment. What one does *not* do in mathematics is to take a very complicated problem, make a wild—or even an educated—guess at the answer, and then fiddle the working-out so as to obtain that answer. No—the problem is posed, the working-out is done with absolute logic and precision, and *then* the answer is obtained. If these steps are followed, however surprising it may seem, the answer will be the correct one.

Now let us transpose this argument into theatrical terms.

What one does *not* do in the theater is to take a very complicated problem (the text), make a wild—or even an educated—guess at the answer (how you will portray your character), and then fiddle the working-out (cut or gloss over certain lines, actions, clues in the text) so as to obtain that answer. No—the problem is posed, the working-out is done with absolute logic and precision, and *then* the answer is obtained. If these steps are followed, however surprising it may seem, the answer will be a correct one.

Because we are dealing with human nature and not an exact science, because no one performance can be the definitive one, we have had to substitute "a" for "the" in that last sentence, but otherwise the method holds true.

It is when the actor makes a rash decision about the character he is to portray and bends everything in the text to that end that cardboard characters appear on our stages, the actor is forced into playing attitudes rather than truths, and the whole exercise becomes weary, stale, flat, and unprofitable.

In this way, a scholarly understanding of a play can sometimes get in the way of an actor's performance. If you come to Hamlet with a certain amount of knowledge about revenge tragedy, you will already have cast Hamlet as the interesting hero, the wronged prince supplanted by a murderous and evil uncle, Claudius. But, as an actor playing Claudius, you can't do this; you have to go to the text to find out who Claudius is. You cannot portray a quality, only a person; and that person will only come to life as you rehearse and explore and understand. The audience needs to see people, not attitudes. It is not up to the actor to judge a character, only to create one; otherwise, instead of a story about people, the audience is presented with a fable about puppets.

No person—and, therefore, no fictional character—is bad in his own eyes. I don't suppose many of us are unfortunate enough to be acquainted with somebody really evil and depraved, but even if we were it is doubtful whether we would recognize him by his habit of slinking around with his head sunk on his shoulders, a curled lip, slit eyes, and a habit of going "heh, heh" to himself when he thought nobody was listening.

Let's look at ourselves. When we sin, however badly we do so, isn't it always justifiable in our own minds? The perks we bring home from work and the time we spend on lunch are both quite justifiable; they are our right. If we lose our tempers, well, we were provoked—"they" went too far, "they" were asking for it—it was righteous indignation. Trivial examples, yes, but that is where it all begins. Everyone can justify his own actions, however bad they are. And how often do you read in the papers, when a murderer or a rapist has been convicted, that his neighbors cannot believe it was possible—a quiet, kind man who thought the world of his dog, always paid his bills on time, and listened to classical music?

Every evildoer has as many friends as you or I, and they love him and respect him. Why, then, can we always see through a stage villain? Because the actor is not playing the truth; he is resorting to caricature or attitude.

Woe to the actor who plays Macbeth, for instance, in the light of the play's ending. What an attractive man he must have been: a national hero, a brilliant soldier, a good and faithful husband, generous, fearless, open, loved and respected by everyone, including the king. To get to the truth of Macbeth, one needs to keep that image of him firmly in mind before one starts on the "heh, heh, heh" and the slit eyes. To understand him one needs to realize that it was not so much ambition that was his undoing as an over-active imagination. To put it in modern terms, he was a man who, one day, read his horoscope in the newspaper and could believe in such things . . .

The actor must *always* reject secondhand ideas, techniques, prejudices, and presuppositions and start with the truth of the text.

It is worth remembering that, for the actor, the words are the starting point; for the writer, the words are the finishing point. What this means is that whatever impulse of action, motive, or characterization provoked this particular scene in the writer's mind, it found its expression in these words. The actor's job is to work backward from the result (the words he is given to speak) to the cause (the impulse which caused the character to speak at all). The words, if you like, are only the tip of an iceberg, and it is that iceberg which you are trying to throw at the audience. The words are only part of the means by which you can do this. Silences can be just as eloquent. Tone, gesture, movement, stillness—all these have their parts to play.

Now, even the most self-confessedly naturalistic of plays doesn't obey the rules of reality which govern our everyday life, but the rules of art. A play is selective; the writer has chosen to show certain things and not to show others. What it shows may look very real in the sense that it is perhaps raw, crude, funny, recognizable, believable; but the important thing is that it is not random. Everything that happens on stage is significant, and all the detail provided by the actors should be significant, too. The actors have to be totally in control of what they are doing. This does not mean that they act by numbers, recreating slavishly the same performance night after night without a hair's breadth of deviation; it means that any addition or subtraction, any new vein of creativity that they open up for themselves or one another should be purposeful, fruitful, and significant.

In practice this means not so much the addition of what is significant, but the omission of what is insignificant. Those in the audience do not need to be told; they naturally assume that everything that happens on the stage is deliberate. Everything that is done, every word, every gesture, every movement, every noise contributes, as it does in music, to make up the full picture. If, therefore, accidental things are happening on the stage, this picture is going to be confused and blurred. If the stage is buzzing with insignificant twitching of legs, scratchings of arms, flickerings of eyes trying to pick out a girlfriend in the audience, and foldings and unfoldings of uncontrollable arms, how can attention be focused on the important things that are happening?

Within the discipline of stillness, however, a tiny movement can make a point that it would take a hundred words to put across. A girl is talking animatedly to a man. As she does so, he removes a thread from her jacket, rolls it between finger and thumb, and drops it to the floor. A gesture that says a lot, but needs to be set amid stillness. A cough delivered in the middle of a pause can be significant, but not if the actor has been coughing and snuffling his way through the previous act and a half without noticing it.

The instinct of people who are not at home on the stage is to keep moving, to shift from foot to foot, to watch everything going on, to walk needlessly around the furniture, and to gesture a great deal. It is a wrong instinct; to watch a play where that is happening is like trying to read a letter that someone has scribbled over. The meaning may be in there somewhere, but it is hardly worth trying to get at it. Life is actually stiller than we imagine. Watch people having a conversation; they don't move very much. There is no need to keep finding reasons for movement on the stage. Some movement may be necessary, some may be helpful, but standing still or sitting still can happen much more often and for longer periods of time than we think.

There is, however, something which happens a great deal in reality and which can be used to great effect on stage—that is, to have a conversation while occupied at a task that has nothing to do with the conversation at all. A couple, for instance, can be tidying up a room as they talk; two people could be having a conversation while engrossed in reading magazines. One man might be cleaning shoes while another looks on; one might be building a model ship. Sometimes these secondary activities are useful for livening up a part of a play that, for some reason, has become difficult to make spontaneous; occasionally the activity itself could have an ironic function, as when a husband and wife are engaged in preparing a sumptuous meal while questioning the motives of Band Aid or a relief organization. Unsubtle perhaps, but you see the point.

Such secondary activities can help motivation and character. While playing the part of a doctor in charge of a psychiatric clinic, I had to interrogate a patient about his political and religious activities. It was more threatening to him and made it harder for him to think clearly if I gave him a medical examination while doing so. Casual questions delivered at the same time as a thump on the back, a whipping up of the shirt tail or a cold spatula on the tongue are disturbing for both patient and audience.

Even if these secondary activities will not fit into the play, they can be useful mind-openers for experiment during rehearsal when a scene needs to be reworked. Try the scene while playing *Monopoly*, putting on a scuba outfit, trying to listen to a talk on the radio, or looking for a lost cufflink.

Spontaneity is the most difficult quality to achieve on stage. In our normal daily life, when we say or do anything, we do not know what is going to happen next. When the doorbell rings, we do not know who it is. When a letter comes, we cannot know what is in it. On stage we *do* know all these things, and yet we mustn't. Often the very first read-through of a play has a quality which is very difficult to reclaim during rehearsal. For at that elementary stage the words really are fresh; we really are meeting the other characters for the first time; we don't know what is going to happen, and any small fluffs of misreadings are amply made up for by the sense of adventure, the delight of giving and taking, of corporate creativity.

The question, of course, is how to regain that spontaneity, and the answer has been more than hinted at in the previous paragraph. It was fresh the first time because we really asked questions and we really listened to the answers; we went through a *real* process of giving and receiving as we talked and listened. That is what made it work, and that is what will make it work again. The actor you don't believe is the one who comes out with his line at the required time; the actor you do believe is the one who, because he has really been listening, has really got a reply to make or a question to ask, not just another piece to fit into a preordained verbal jigsaw.

One of the enemies of spontaneity is the desire we have to make every line a telling one, full of import. We seldom, if ever, do this in real conversation, but it is a common fault on the stage. Yes, of course every line is significant as we have just been discussing, but that is not the same as thinking that every line must be delivered with great weight and sense of purpose. Some lines are significant of the fact that we are in a different world, that we cannot think of anything to say, that we are nonplussed, embarrassed, playing for time, and many other forms of temporary incoherence. These lines can often gain by being thrown away, mumbled, split up with hesitations, or glossed over quickly. In doing this, other lines are thereby thrown into relief. Take these, for instance.

> *Charles:*   He's probably just stopped to see somebody on the way. He'll be all right. He's a good driver. What's for dinner?

If the first three sentences are spoken with real conviction in a genuine effort to comfort and reassure, each one will have slightly more weight than the previous one, and there will be a need for a smallish pause between each sentence to see if the desired consolation has taken place. With this method of playing the speech the last sentence becomes an anticlimax; such an anticlimax, in fact, that it sheds suspicion on the earlier attempts to comfort.

The other way to play the speech is to throw off the first three sentences without any pause at all. This tells the audience that Charles is not worried (or not interested) and he doesn't believe that the person he is talking to is worried either. Then there must be a longer pause before the last sentence. This is the question he is really working toward!

Additionally, the first method demands that Charles should look at the person he is speaking to; it would be very unnatural not to. The second method, however, requires that he should definitely *not* look, at least until "What's for dinner?" and not necessarily even then.

In studying a part it is helpful to go through the lines working out exactly what the important lines are with regard to motive and plot, and to separate them from others which are just social noises, small talk, habitual clichés. These can carry less weight and be used to make your character real, human, and interesting. Look for the line or lines in each of your speeches which carry the point of the whole speech, which contain the essence of what the character is trying to say at that particular point, and use the other lines to frame them.

Stanislavski is very helpful on this subject, what he calls "Units and Objectives."[1] He breaks a play down into its main component parts, and then each of those parts into units. Now, if the actor sees each of those units as something that has to be gained or won, rather like a soldier occupying strategic points during a battle, he will be able to find a through-line for each scene which will help him to understand how much weight or lightness to expend on each line.

As actors we should always be asking ourselves the question, "Why am I saying that?" and other related questions such as, "Why do I use that particular phrasing?" "Why do I say that instead of . . . ?" and "What am I really getting at here?" Because a good writer knows that people very often don't say what they mean, they cloak the real questions and feelings—they pretend to be at ease when they are not, they cover embarrassment with rudeness which they do not mean, they hide anger behind a mask of ultra-politeness.

An actor must be ready to meet and understand all these dis-simulations in a text. They are particularly invaluable when trying to find the truth behind a classic play which has been done over and over again. Look at the text, think, analyze, always be asking "Why?" even if the answer turns out to be the obvious one.

In a similar way, an actor can often find a lot of creative fuel in playing against the emotion that seems to be required of him. If, for instance, a stage direction says, "He is now becoming very frightened," instead of playing the fear that the playwright has asked for, beginning to tremble, to look around nervously and wipe sweat from the brow, all of which are clichés and, unless done brilliantly, will look stagey and contrived, the actor could become suddenly very calm, controlled, and quietly logical. Because the first thing that people do when they are conscious of fear is try to hide it, try to pull themselves together and fight against it.

Again, to become extremely careful and precise with one's diction and movements is a much more subtle and realistic way of portraying drunkenness than the usual slurred speech and uncontrollable stagger.

These are just some of the ways in which the actor can help the audience to understand what Stanislavski calls the subtext, and what I have visualized as the iceberg beneath the surface of the play: it is this iceberg, this subtext, that makes us say the words we say, that makes us do the things we do. The words and actions are not ends in themselves, they are revelations—huge ones, tiny ones, distorted ones, oblique ones—of the iceberg, the Idea of the play.

What does this mean for the actor? It means, first of all, that merely speaking the lines clearly and not bumping into the furniture are scarcely even a start toward the real work of acting; one expects that, at least—just as one expects a painter to be able to balance his canvas on the easel before he starts, or a musician to be able to open the case in which he keeps his instrument.

In the next chapter we will look in more detail at some of the elements of stagecraft, some ideas to use as basic blocks on which to build a technique; but I want to end this one with some discussion about the main weapon in the actor's armory—thought. Castaways on *Desert Island Discs* often speak of the difficulty of having to restrict themselves to only eight records from a whole world of music. If I were forced to reduce this book to only eight words, those eight words would be "Think, think, think, think, think, think, think, think!"

When people talk to you, do you sit there blankly until they have finished and then reply? No. As they talk, you are thinking. You may be thinking about what they are saying, or you may be thinking more about the person who is talking; you may even be thinking, "I wish this idiot would finish so that I can have my say," but something is going on in your head. The same must happen on stage. There is, at rehearsal, many a needless cry of, "How should I react to that?" If the actor in question had been listening, genuinely listening, to what was being said to him and thinking about that rather than trying to remember his next line or worrying about a move in a previous scene, he would, in most cases, know how he should react.

Real thought does our acting for us. You can sit on an empty stage for minutes on end and hold an audience's attention if you are really thinking. On the other hand, I have watched a telephone conversation on stage during which the actor never gave more than two seconds for the voice on the other end to have its say. Disaster. Not only was the illusion of reality destroyed, but, because of that, the actor became annoying in the eyes of the audience—they began to dislike him (though I doubt whether many of them could have said why) and he began to fake reactions to words which were not and could never have been spoken. If he had thought what he was doing, he would never have committed such a basic error.

It is thought that tells us whether we need a pause before we speak or whether we come straight in; it is thought that fills the stage when nothing else is going on; it is thought that will tell you how to inflect a line; it is thought that will tell you when to move and when to stand still; it is thought that is responsible for good timing and, therefore, for successful comedy. When you are in the grip of an emotion—that is, when you are completely occupied mentally—you can do anything you like on the stage; you can move anywhere, gesticulate, knock things over, contort your body, all things which would be very, very hard to tackle cold. Try it. Get really angry, and you will suddenly find that you are liberated from all constraints including embarrassment; everything suddenly works. Why? Because you are thinking: you are so lost in the thought and feeling that the emotion has produced that you are no longer self-conscious. You don't have to think about how to be-have, your thoughts are ahead of you and are making you behave.

Reactions on stage are a result of thought forcing the body into an expression. If that is kept in mind, then there is less danger of the awful kinds of stock reaction that we so often see. When an actor is surprised, his eyes stare, his jaw drops, he turns to the audience, he turns back to the other actor, he leans back in his chair, he signifies nothing except his own lack of thought and observation.

Go and surprise somebody now, and watch what they do. Almost certainly the first they do will be nothing. They will freeze all movement for a second or so while their *thoughts* try to grasp the information that has just been imparted. What happens immediately after that will depend on the sort of person they are, but the first thing will not be movement but stillness, the stillness of thought.

Genuine reactions are nearly always less than we imagine them to be. It is a bad exercise to try portraying an emotion in a vacuum; standing in front of the bedroom mirror rehearsing perplexity, joy, sudden grief, and so on, because we tend to concentrate on the emotion rather than on the thought which caused it. Just as words are the end product of the writer's thoughts, so reactions should be the end product of an actor's thoughts. We don't have to put on reactions so long as we are genuinely listening and genuinely thinking. Most reactions are only just perceptible; when they *do* come out, they tend to come out in the whole body rather than in the face. Fingers twist, chairs scrape, noses are rubbed, the torso sways perhaps, but the face usually tries to disguise the emotion.

Television has a lot to answer for in this matter of reactions. When a character has, for instance, received bad news, a hack director will come in close on that character's face. Well, the poor guy has to do something; realizing that a genuine reaction is not going to be seen, he resorts to a cliché and lets his face crumple.

Just count the number of scenes in soap operas and TV series where the final picture is a slow fade on the face of some unfortunate person expected to portray triumphal disdain mixed with guilt and a certain amount of apprehension; or nobility in grief touched with regret and yet stoical acceptance. It is hardly acting; it is more like eyebrow choreography, and it is always the actor who gets the blame.

Thinking can also help you with physical movement on stage. It should not be necessary to say it, but I will say it anyway—a movement on stage should always be made for a purpose which is discernible to the audience. This does not include such demands from the director as, "It's getting a bit static, darling; could you do a cross at this point?" If you are standing by a table downstage left and the director wants you to move to the mantelpiece, stage right, there has got to be a reason for it in the mind of the character. This is what is known as motivation. Motivation and movement are not usually too much of a problem in a good play. In Willy Russell's play *Educating Rita*, for instance, there is plenty of excuse for movement from Rita in the first scene: she is young, nervous, out of her depth, desperate to prove herself, and feels intellectually inferior. Plenty of scope there; but what the actress must *not* do is give herself these generalizations as reasons for a move. An actor has to work with concrete reasons, not with generalizations. "Nervousness" is not a real motivation, whereas "wanting to get out of the tutor's line of sight for a moment" *is* real motivation. It is still a result of nervousness, yes, but it is a concrete reason rather than a vague idea. Try always to find a definite, positive reason for moving; it could be to look more closely at a word-processor because you have never seen one before, it could be to straighten a clock on a shelf, to look at a picture, to try out a swivel-chair. Nothing is more distracting than a vague wafting about the stage; nothing is more satisfying than purposeful movement against a confident stillness.

Thus, when you make a move it is a bit like maneuvering a car. Remember the sequence? Mirror, signal, go. On stage it is look, think, move. Maybe while you are talking you catch sight of the picture; you think, "That looks interesting . . ." and then you cross to look at it. While you're about it you might also decide whether you have crossed to see what the picture is of, or how old it is, or who painted it. No, the audience will not pick that up, but *you* will know precisely what you are doing, and that will give you the security you need.

This is what rehearsal is for. It is to work through the thinking processes, to give you the absolute security of knowing who you are, why you say the things you do, and what mental distances you travel during the play.

One last thing about thought. We have seen how thought makes us say the words that we do say, how it carries on while others are speaking, how it may sometimes prevent us from replying immediately or provoke us to interrupt, how it may freeze our movement or compel movement. But it is also worth considering why we ever stop speaking on stage. Now that might seem like an odd question; we stop because the dramatist has given us no more words. What I mean is, when you start speaking does your character *know* that he is going to stop there, or has he got more to say that he would have said if X had not come in with his comment? When he speaks again, does he interrupt X? Is what he says this time a continuation of his first thought, or is it a result of what X has said that he takes this particular line? Suppose (and you can try this at rehearsals) X does not come in with his line? How will you continue? Or won't you? Very often, when you watch an actor, you can tell when he is coming to the end of a speech. Should you be able to? It is not something to generalize about, but it is worth asking the question when you come to play a part.

There is also, of course, an allied question: what happens after a scene has finished? The audience will gather what happens next;

Charles goes off to have a showdown with David, or, to choose a real instance, Banquo goes off to tell his wife that he is going away on business for the day and taking Fleance with him. The writer does not show the scene because it is unimportant except in as much as it has to happen for the plot to unfold, or perhaps because it is too difficult to write. But it is important for the actor. Next time he appears he has been through that experience; he has traveled, mentally, that bit further than the last time we saw him. Sometimes that will not make any noticeable difference, sometimes it will make a huge difference and the actor needs to be a changed man; sometimes it will make a tiny difference—perhaps the actor will arrive out of breath, or in a very thoughtful mood, or with scarcely concealed delight. Each case needs to be considered on its merits.

If you forget everything else about this book, remember at least to base your performance on the truth of the text and not on preconceived ideas, to do nothing without purpose, to listen properly and respond to what you hear, to think. And the greatest of these is to think.

Notes

1. Stanislavski, *An Actor Prepares.* New York: Theatre Arts Books, 1970.

3

Stagecraft

Everything that happens on the stage must be convincing to the actor himself, to his associates and to the spectators. It must inspire belief in the possibility, in real life, of emotions analogous to those being experienced on the stage by the actor . . . Clichés will fill up every empty spot in a role which is not already solid with living feeling. Moreover, they often rush in ahead of feeling, and bar the road.

Constantin Stanislavski, *An Actor Prepares*

*T*he following hints and wrinkles will not help you to become an actor; the most that they can do is to clear the way so that real acting can start. They are techniques intended to help you, and the actors around you, believe more firmly in what you are doing, erase bad habits, and prepare the ground for imagination and inspiration to put forth shoots.

Acting is, ultimately, learning how to be a real person. Nobody can teach that. We do not have techniques for being the people we are, but we do have friends who can rebuke or encourage, we have architects who give us a place to live, agriculturists who feed us physically, writers who feed us mentally, a faith which feeds us spiritually, and a mother and father who teach us to walk and talk without stumbling. That's what stagecraft is: a theatrical parent. It provides an atmosphere and a safeguard for growth, but we have to do the growing ourselves and in our own way.

Yourself

This is the material you have to work with. It is a limitation that cannot be overcome. But exactly how limited it is depends on what you feed it and how you exercise it. You can always use less than you are; you can never use more. So the more fully you live, think, and experience, the greater will be your range and capacity as an actor. Thus, all other things being equal, the older an actor is, the better he will be for he will have more knowledge and experience to draw on. He will have met more people, seen more countries, read more books, heard more music, been through more difficulties, had more pain and more delight. Private qualities always spill over into public art.

It is worth stressing again that more can always become less; less cannot easily become more. An intelligent man will be more easily capable of being thick-witted than a stupid man of being intelligent; a man who can walk with grace and poise can easily reduce that to a shamble, but the man who naturally shambles cannot reduce that to poise. So we must learn to make the most of our strengths and do our best to convert our weaknesses. If we have the beginnings of a particular talent—an ear for regional accents, a gymnastic ability, a capacity for stand-up comedy—let us develop it; and let us learn whatever skills are there for learning—dancing, singing, playing an instrument, fencing, conjuring, riding a unicycle; and let us not neglect to grow inside us the fruit of the Spirit, for qualities such as patience, kindness, gentleness, and self-control are as essential to an actor as any of his physical skills.

It cannot be repeated too often: our acting is limited by our experience. The man who does not know what subtlety is cannot portray a subtle character; the man who does not know what

gentleness is cannot portray a gentle character. You bring yourself
to everything; empty vessels make empty sounds.

Learning Words

I have changed my mind about this matter. I used to think that it
was better not to learn lines in a vacuum, to wait until a few days
into rehearsal when one could see how the play was taking shape
and how all the other actors were playing their parts. I am still
convinced that it is *easier* to learn this way. Having gone through a
scene six or seven times, trying different things, playing the scene
in different ways, when you come to learn the lines you find that
most of them have stuck without your having to make any effort
at all: mere repetition has fixed them. But I am no longer convinced
that this is the point.

The early period of rehearsal is the time when all the very basic
decisions about moves and characters are made. If you come to
rehearsal having studied your character and knowing all the lines,
you are in a better position to decide what moves and ideas are
right. You will have some idea, even if not a finished one, of how
you want to play the part; you will make decisions and suggestions
from a position of knowledge, not of sheer guesswork. If you do
not do this, then all decisions will have to be made by the director,
and directors, on the whole, are much better at responding to a
positive contribution from an actor than to his helplessness.

You will be able to listen properly to what the rest of the cast is
giving you if you have not got your head stuck in the book and a
mind stuck in wondering what is going to happen next. In short,
you can be creative at an earlier stage and give yourself more time
for detail and polish.

The argument against coming to rehearsal with all lines learned
is that, having learned them alone, it will be more difficult to
change your fixed ideas if, as is likely, they need to be adapted to
other people's ideas and needs. If that is so, if you are the sort of

person who, once he has got something into his head, cannot easily be persuaded to change it, then you must be honest with yourself about it and either change or not learn your lines until later. But actors, on the whole, have to be a pretty adaptable bunch, willing and able to experiment and to change whatever needs changing right up to the end of rehearsals or even later. And, after all, if you do have to change one or two things that you thought were fixed, well—it is only one or two; that must be easier than learning forty or fifty new things.

Rehearsals

Rehearsals are for the benefit of the actors. A play is a bit like a soufflé: it takes a certain amount of time to cook, and if you open the oven door halfway through the process to show off how well it is coming along, it will almost certainly be ruined.

Do not bring Aunt Ethel or your dad to rehearsals. Even more important, do not bring your boyfriend or girlfriend. You will be tempted to show off rather than work. Rehearsals are incredibly tedious occupations for all those involved, and, with an audience even of only one or two, you will instinctively want to perform long before performance is a possibility. The work you should have done will not get done, and the work you have already done may well be spoiled.

Acting is a very courageous activity. In trying to get to the truth of a part, an actor sometimes has to be sacrificially honest about his own thoughts and behavior and shortcomings. He makes himself vulnerable. This vulnerability must be respected by the rest of the cast if people are not going to get hurt. The rehearsal room, therefore, must be a safe place, a place where, if secrets are told, they are kept, if difficult things are revealed they are not gossipped about. If this privacy is invaded then it must be with the complete approval of everybody concerned, or actors are going to clam up and may never dare open themselves again.

The other thing to say about rehearsals is that they are for the benefit of the actors who are rehearsing at the time, not for the rest of the cast sitting around drinking coffee.

I am all for actors staying in the rehearsal room and watching what goes on when they are not involved in a scene. It can do nothing but good for them to see what is going into other people's performances. It may teach them something about acting; it will certainly teach them something about the play; and when they come to do some work they will be more fit for it than if they had been lying out in the sun or (my own personal distraction) sniffing around second-hand bookstores for half an hour. But they should remember that they are not there to make comments or criticisms unless they are invited to do so by the director or the cast, and they are not there to distract or provide entertainment. Occasionally an actor, knowing that he is going to make an embarrassing mess of a difficult scene, will prefer to work alone with the director until he has sorted it out for himself. He must be allowed this freedom. Scenes of intense emotion are very difficult to work on while others are sitting around analyzing it all. Actors must feel safe.

Blocking

Blocking means setting the moves and the action of a play, working out where people go and when. What the actor needs to know is why. Most of this has been covered on previous pages, but there are a few other points to make.

Before rehearsals start, the set will have been designed and will be in the process of being constructed and painted. Certain decisions, therefore, about blocking will be preordained. Actors can only exit where there are doors, can only switch on lamps at lamp-switches, and can sit down on chairs only where there are chairs. Within these obvious limitations there is still plenty of scope, and it is a good idea for the actors and the director to work together in deciding how a scene will be moved; the actor knows why he wants to move (or why he doesn't), and the director is the only one who can tell how it looks from the front, and how effective such moves are. Almost always, the blocking that is roughed out at the beginning is just a piece of temporary scaffolding. As the building takes shape, as characters develop, scenes shift in emphasis and relationships become richer, so the scaffolding will be reconstructed. At the first rehearsals, therefore, if a move still doesn't seem quite right, or you are unhappy about sitting at a certain point, don't worry too much about it; it can change when you come to work on that part of the play in more detail and get to know precisely what is needed. Let it go for the moment. Better to have something that is almost efficient than nothing at all.

When you compare, say, a French's Acting Edition of a play by Agatha Christie with any edition of a Shakespeare play, one huge difference is immediately noticeable: the Shakespeare has practically no stage directions and no indication of scenery apart from a vague "Somewhere in Illyria" or "Another Part of the Wood." The Agatha Christie will have a photograph of the set, a plan of it, a list of properties and special effects, and the stage directions will be given in the most minute detail. Now these can be helpful, but they do not have to be followed slavishly if you feel you want to do something different; they are simply a record of how the play was set and blocked when it was done previously. Most editions give you what the author wrote. Shakespeare gets the prize for brevity; Stoppard gets the prize for wit.

There is a kind of taboo inherited from some theatrical folklore which says that you should never turn your back on an audience. This is nonsense and was discredited long, long ago, but it still seems to hang around in the minds of some who know little else about the theater but have clung on to this gem. If it is natural to turn your back, turn your back; it will make a change from your front if you are on-stage for a long time; and there is no other way of making a dignified exit through the doors upstage center. It may be that the acoustics of the hall dictate that you do not talk while your back is turned, and it is certainly difficult to concentrate on speech that comes from an invisible face, but that is a different matter.

Masking

This simply means getting in the way so that one of the characters on-stage cannot be seen by the audience. Now, if you take a moment's thought, you will realize that once there are more than two people on-stage—unless they are standing in a straight line, which looks horribly unnatural—someone is almost bound to be at least partially masked from one or two in the audience. This doesn't matter. What does matter is that a character should be clearly seen when he has anything important to contribute, whether vocally or silently. If you are being masked, the person doing the masking must by definition be downstage from you and therefore unable to see that he is masking you. He could, of course, be doing it deliberately. In either case the remedy is quite simply to move. If he, in turn, moves again so as to mask you, you can be pretty sure he is doing it deliberately. Unless you want to turn the play into a kind of medieval dance, you are probably better off sticking where you are and having a word with him later. From your stock of love, joy, peace, gentleness, and self-control, of course.

Upstaging

Masking could, I suppose, be called a form of "downstaging." Upstaging is to do something distracting so as to take the focus of attention off the main characters and onto something totally negligible. It tends to happen upstage, hence the name, so that it cannot properly be seen by the actors whose performance it is destroying.

There is a school of thought which says that upstaging is impossible if the other actors are really doing their stuff; the audience will be riveted, and any distraction will be to no avail. It must be admitted that there is a lot of truth in that, and many a mediocre actor has blown the whistle on some good work by an excellent actor simply because his own performance was not strong enough to cope with the competition. However, noises will certainly distract and can destroy an actor's timing and can kill an audience's laughter. Activity on its own probably will not upstage, unless, of course, the actor performing is determined that it should.

The actors should, of course, like orchestral musicians, be sensitive to one another's performances; they should be aware of what they are doing and how it is affecting the play.

There was a famous actress who used to boast that she could upstage an actor even when she was not on-stage. How? Well, she did it one night. Just before she made her exit, she balanced a fragile glass on the very edge of a small table. Whatever the leading man did after that, you can be sure that the audience's eyes never left that glass.

Character Changes

Do you always behave in exactly the same way whatever company you are in? No, you don't. Nor do I. We are all chameleons to a certain extent; we change our behavior to fit or deliberately *not* to fit whatever is going on around us. Some people always make us act aggressively, some people relax us, some people bring out the pedant in us, some people make us defensive. It must be the same for characters in plays, and yet how often we see an actor playing the same quality in every scene. He is always prickly, or always fearful, or always undemonstrative. This can get boring, and it is not true to life. Just as pace and vocal quality have to be varied, so characters have to reveal different facets of themselves.

There will always be scope for this in a well-written play. Some characters are so well-drawn that they can even act out of character without becoming unbalanced or fragmented.

Look for the sections in a script which will allow you to push your characterization just that bit further; tell us a little more; make him *really* interesting. When you start doing that, or at least experimenting with the idea, you will find that it evokes interesting responses in the other actors as well which can lead to further developments, further possibilities.

Convince the Actors

Who are you trying to convince with your acting? The audience? No. Well, yes and no. First of all you must convince yourself. Look at what you are doing, how you are thinking, the way you are talking. Is it truthful? Do you believe it yourself, or are you just saying the lines in a beautiful or a "meaningful" way with some very fine gestures and perhaps some dramatic pauses or sighs? Come on, now, be honest; are you dishing up clichés, or are you telling the truth? Is this really what the character is about, or are you just skating through, giving us a cipher rather than a person? Do you make speeches, or do you just say things? The point is, if you are not honest with yourself, if *you* are not convinced, you will not convince the other actors; and if they are not convinced they will have to fake their responses to you. So you fake, and they fake back, and how is the audience going to see the truth beneath all those little forgeries?

Don't set out to convince the audience; don't perform; don't say, "Look at this! Look what I've managed to do with *these* lines!" Simply go for the truth and convince the rest of the cast. That's what will grip the audience; then you really will be acting for them.

Of course you are not doing a private performance; for a start, you have to be heard, you have to be seen and understood. But that is where you end up, not where you begin. Do not be misled into thinking that this rapport between the actors is a form of self-indulgence: just the opposite—it is extremely hard work. The self-in-

dulgence would be to show off, to go around performing like mad
and enjoying yourself.

Attention

We have stressed in the previous chapter how important it is to
listen and to listen properly, not just to wait for the end of a speech
and then come in with the next line. Now let us add a layer or two
to that thought.

There is not just one way of listening. Sometimes we listen to
what is said and reply to that thought. This is the most straightforward kind of listening. Here is some Pinter:

> *Ben:*   Go on, go and light it.
> *Gus:*   Eh?
> *Ben:*   Go and light it.
> *Gus:*   Light what?
> *Ben:*   The kettle.
> *Gus:*   You mean the gas.
> *Ben:*   Who does?
> *Gus:*   You do.
> *Ben:*   (his eyes narrowing) What do you mean, I mean
>   the gas?
> *Gus:*   Well, that's what you mean, don't you? The gas.
> *Ben:*   (powerfully) If I say go and light the kettle I
>   mean go and light the kettle.
> *Gus:*   How can you light a kettle?
> *Ben:*   It's a figure of speech! Light the kettle. It's a
>   figure of speech!
> *Gus:*   I've never heard it.
> *Ben:*   Light the kettle! It's common usage!
> *Gus:*   I think you've got it wrong.
> *Ben:*   (menacing) What do you mean?

> Gus: They say put on the kettle.
> Ben: (taut) Who says?[1]

Both characters are giving complete attention to what the other is saying. But there are other forms of listening. Sometimes we half-hear or don't want to hear, so that when we speak we are merely carrying on with our own thought. There is quite a bit of that in this passage from N.F. Simpson:

> Bro: It's a fourteenth-century brass rocking chair in
>   the form of a set of Regency-style false teeth
>   made to look like an old Byzantine bell-pull.
> Middie: As if we haven't got enough clutter.
> Bro: It's the one thing that corner's always wanted, I
>   think. To take the bleakness off it. Something
>   hanging down.
> Middie: What happens if somebody gives it a tug?
>   Accidentally. I suppose the whole lot comes
>   down. Ceiling and all.
> Bro: There's no need to give it a tug.
> Middie: You get an idea in your head, and instead of
>   stopping to think, you go out and come
>   home with something like that. That's going
>   to be a perpetual eyesore. *And* a nuisance.
>   When I'm dusting.
> Bro: A lot of people would like it. It adds a touch of
>   distinction.
> Middie: It's all right if you've got flunkeys in the house.
>   To answer it. What's the good of it to me?
>   And chambermaids.
> Bro: A chambermaid wouldn't answer a bell like that,
>   Middie.
> Middie: Here, there and everywhere. Getting under your
>   feet.

Bro:	What?
Middie:	Up to our necks in butlers and pantrymen and I don't know what else. Trooping into the room every time the bell rings.
Bro:	But . . .
Middie:	Holding their hands out for tips every minute of the day and night. When you want to get on.
Bro:	This is a *disused* bell pull, Middie!
Middie:	Smoking on duty.
Bro:	It's past it now. As far as summoning anybody is concerned. It's purely decorative.
Middie:	Powdered footmen under your feet.
Bro:	Middie.
Middie:	Under gardeners. Vying with each other.[2]

Bro is certainly listening to Middie quite consciously, but Middie takes no notice of Bro after the first three or four exchanges.

Sometimes—here is yet another way of listening—we do actually listen to what the other person is saying, but we are more interested in the speaker than his words. Again, it is a matter of digging down to the truth, not just taking the lines at their surface value—that will only produce surface performances.

So: work out exactly where your attention lies—is it on what the other character is saying? Is it on the other character himself? Is it on what you are thinking about or looking at? Find that point of attention, and the lines will virtually look after themselves.

Eye Contact

When we look at people we look into their eyes. We don't hold their gaze unswervingly for twenty minutes—or only in exceptional circumstances—but we do look at them, and we must look at them on-stage. A lot of thought happens in eye-to-eye contact. To avoid it is to go dead. There is nothing worse than trying to hold a conversation with someone who is resolutely looking over your left shoulder or at one of your ears. It makes you feel as if you are about to be assassinated or as if parts of your body are growing to an abnormal size or taking on an extraordinary hue. It is, in short, uncomfortable.

The usual reason for avoidance of eye contact between people is embarrassment or guilt. If you are embarrassed about being on-stage, then you should not be there. If your *character* is embarrassed, well, that is a different kettle of fish.

Exits and Entrances

One of the most epidemic faults among inexperienced actors is to come on-stage, take up a position, and then start acting. Usually the first part of the maneuver is undertaken with bowed shoulders and purposeful gait, or with shifting eyes and a smirk. More experienced actors start acting as soon as they are in view of the audience. Real actors start well before they even begin to move on to the stage.

The point is that the play is continuing off-stage as well as on-stage. When characters appear, they are coming *to* somewhere *from* somewhere; they are in a particular state of mind. They are not just appearing from some limbo to exist for a few minutes and then disappear back into the void. But all too often it looks as if precisely this is happening.

No, you have got to have a real life that is going on even when we cannot see it. We are back to thought again. *Think:* where have you been? What was it like? Who were you with? What did they say? What did you say? How far have you traveled mentally since you were last on-stage? Did you know you were coming here? *Did you know these people were going to be here?* Why are you here?

The answer to all these questions should be in your mind before you come on-stage. Not all of them will be conscious, of course, especially by the time you actually come to perform, but you will have to make them conscious at some point during the rehearsal in order to give you the motivation to enter and do what you have to do.

You may even be halfway through saying something or doing something as you appear: stubbing out an illegal cigarette, putting on a jacket, finishing off a piece of sponge-cake, or anything that without being fatuous helps you to feel the life of the situation you have just left.

In the same way, when you leave the stage you are also going somewhere. There is one small practical problem involved here; as you leave the stage you may well be walking into an inky blackness. You'll have to get used to that. You must not drop your head and grope your way off the stage. You must make sure, to the best of your ability, that there will be nothing in the way, and then trust. Only when you are safely in the wings dare you stop thinking in character.

Prepare your exits carefully during rehearsals. It is very disconcerting to deliver a wonderful exit line and then find that you have got eight paces to tread before you can actually leave the stage. The play becomes a pancake, and any eggs leftover from the pancake will be put on your face. Sometimes a slow exit is good and necessary, but it is usually the other way around.

Here's one final tip for when you are performing a series of sketches interspersed with blackouts. When the blackout comes, the contrast between the previous brightness and the sudden darkness will effectively blind you for several seconds. If you close your eyes gently—do *not* screw them up or you will destroy the point of the whole exercise—just as the blackout comes, give it a second, and then open them, you will find that your vision has been able to adjust to the darkness much more quickly and you can walk off-stage and *see* yourself trip over the stage weights.

Pauses

Sorry, but it has to be repeated. Pauses are holes full of thought; little breeding grounds for new possibilities, for decisions, for stocktaking, for mental travel. They are not gaps. Every pause must be full of something; empty ones are the onset of theatrical death.

During the war when necessities were rationed and many things were hard to obtain, posters were put up asking, "Is Your Journey Really Necessary?" Theatrically speaking, time is rationed and theatrical truth is not easy to come by or to sustain; we ought each to have a mental poster in our heads asking, "Is Your Pause Really Necessary?"

Pauses can be very significant. We have seen how silence can be as telling as words or actions; but they can be overdone. Pauses can easily become clichés. We cannot find the truth, or we cannot be bothered to work at it, so we pause and hope that the audience will fill it with the significance that is missing. Of course they cannot. Pauses can be indicative of still waters running deep, but they can also be indicative of deep waters closing over the actor's head.

Remember, too, that when you pause it is like a car drawing up at traffic lights: everybody else has to stop until you move again. Never pause without necessity; and watch out, too, for bad writers using pauses in the same way—to cover up lack of real thought and significance.

Eating and Drinking

Actors are sometimes called upon, though not very frequently, to eat on-stage. It is not as easy as might be imagined. Just as all the other things which, at home, we do easily and without need for a second thought—talking, listening, standing around doing nothing, thinking—are more difficult when they are brought forward into the realm of conscious activity, so is eating.

All too often, the mouth is dry; the food goes round and round and you cannot find a space during which to swallow, and if you could you know it wouldn't go down.

The answer is to make sure the stage manager supplies you with food that is particularly easy to eat and that is not too filling; you won't want to do the rest of the performance on a full stomach. The best foods for this purpose are those which need no chewing and which have plenty of moisture of their own: scrambled eggs, mashed potato, bananas and cream, tomatoes, rice pudding, even pasta shells with plenty of sauce.

There are all sorts of other things one can do, such as using pots of baby food, which is very easy to swallow, of course, or slicing up some segments of orange instead of carrots. At all costs avoid bread, any variety of cookies, pastry, cake, or meat.

Take much smaller mouthfuls than usual; however carefully you work things out, you will find, one night, that you've put a forkful in just as you are about to deliver your big speech. If you have taken only a small mouthful, you can get rid of it quickly and avoid turning your co-stars into something out of Tom and Jerry.

Drinks are wet, so they are easy. But they are easy to spill as well, so be careful; and remember that holding a full glass will show up any shakes or tremblings in your hand. The golden rule is never to drink on an empty lung—by which I mean, if you take a breath *before* you drink and refrain from breathing *while* you drink, you will not choke, cough, or sputter.

Pace and Picking Up Cues

A cue, technically, is anything which signals that you should do something. Normally it is used of the last phrase of one actor's speech which tells the other actor that it is his turn, but it could just as easily be a movement, a piece of music, a change of lighting, or a sound effect. It is not quite an unbreakable rule, but it is worth thinking of it as an unbreakable rule, that cues should be picked up—that is, responded to, without a break. If a pause *has* to be made, it is usually better to pick up the cue and *then* pause rather than pause between cue and reply. Not this:

> *He*:   Are you coming with me, then?
> *She*:   (Pausing to look at him with extreme patience)
>   How many more times do I have to tell you?
>   I've got things to do!

but this:

> *He*:   Are you coming with me, then?
> *She*:   How many more times do I have to tell you!
>   (Pause) I've got things to do!

Now ask yourself whether the pause is really necessary at all. What if one were to run the two sentences together, but speak the second one as if to a dim-witted child?

Actors who persist—and it's usually our old friend, lack of thought—in leaving a beat between the end of one speech and the beginning of another, are liable to affect an audience in the same way as a man who always begins his sentences with "Er . . ." In the end it drives you mad.

Pace is not the same thing as speed. Pace has nothing to do with the speed at which characters speak or move; it has to do with the way in which the play moves itself along. A slow scene, full of pauses and silences, can grip the audience and keep them on the edge of their seats. If it does that, then the pace is right. Music will provide a fair analogy.

A symphony, a concerto, or a suite are all divided up into movements as a play is divided into scenes. Each movement has its proper speed, and is usually in contrast to those which surround it, but each has pace as well which prevents fast movements from becoming a scramble and slow movements from becoming turgid.

When the violins have finished a phrase, perhaps the oboe will pick it up, but not with a gap, or the pace will flag. Listen to the slow movement of Mozart's Piano Concerto K467 in C major, popularized by use in the film *Elvira Madigan*. The speed actually changes from bar to bar, from phrase to phrase, though you would not notice it—the overall pulse or pace remains the same. If, in fact, the movement were played strictly in time to a metronome, it would lose all pace and become unbearably dull.

Pace has to do with energy; a scene can be very slow and very quiet, but crammed with energy. Speed can dazzle, but it is pace that allows you to sit through an hour of theater and feel that you've only been there for fifteen minutes. Time passes at a certain and unchangeable rate; we know that. The fact that some days drag and others seem to flash past is due to pace, to the energy or lack of energy that each called forth.

Thus, pace on-stage is not gained by gabbling or rushing hither and thither; it is gained by the correct use of energy—sometimes potential, sometimes kinetic—by relaxation opposing tension, by a counterpoint of speed, tone, and color.

Cheating

We have already dealt with mental cheating when discussing such concepts as "truth," "listening," and "pauses"; I want now to look briefly at physical cheating on the stage. And what I mean by cheating is performing an action in shorthand. Do you remember the actor on the telephone who alienated his audience by not allowing the guy on the other end to have his say? That is cheating. Ask someone to mime picking up a glass and drinking from it. Chances are that he will clench his fist, bring it up to his mouth, and expel a satisfied "Aaaaaah!" as he removes his fist again. Shorthand. Cheating. When you pick up a glass you grip it near the top, and there should be room between the thumb and fingers for the whole circumference of the rim, which is probably bigger than you think. The hand has to be kept level as you raise the glass or the drink will spill. You don't, finally, bring the glass to your lips, you bring your head forward and your lips to the glass. You don't need to tip much to take quite a big draught, and you certainly don't tip your head back until you are right at the bottom of the glass. The expulsion of air does not take place until *after* the swallow—and seldom even then. It is usually a cliché.

Well, that's what I mean by cheating. It is often done—as in the drinking example—owing to a lack of thought. It is sometimes done for the right reasons, but then, the pathway to some very nasty destinations is paved with good intentions. The actor on the telephone was, perhaps, and mistakenly, merely trying to keep up the pace. Instead of doing that, he destroyed the illusion—the one illusion that it was imperative to keep alive.

You must never cheat on the merely physical things that have to take place. If you are supposed to be ringing a long-distance number, then you must dial eleven digits. Do not worry about the time it takes—and don't be tempted to dial 1-111-111-1111; there's always some smart aleck who can tell the number you have dialed. If you have to read something and comment on it, give yourself time to read it. If you have to write a note, for goodness sake, write it and don't do a three-year-old's drawing of the southerly view from your favorite vacation spot on the Pacific ocean. It's always obvious to the audience if you haven't actually performed these simple tasks properly. You might give the performance of a lifetime, but there's not much point if they all go home muttering that you couldn't possibly have got through to Paris by dialing five digits, or taken down an address in 4.73 seconds.

Corpsing

To corpse is to laugh at the wrong time; to find, suddenly, that the line being spoken or the character you are portraying is very funny. It is doubtful whether the audience will find it funny at all. It is the one certain way to ruin comedy. You will hear people salving their consciences by asserting that the audience loves that sort of thing, but they don't, you know. If a well-known comedian should crack up during a routine, the audience will certainly enjoy it. It is nice to see that one's heroes are human; but don't forget that this is after 482 performances *without* corpsing. Many comedians play themselves playing parts; they keep one foot outside their characterizations, and it is that which is the springboard for much of their humor.

Coleridge referred to the audience's acceptance of theatrical conventions as "a willing suspension of disbelief." They know that what is happening on the stage is not really *true*, they do not actually believe it; and yet, for the duration of the performance, they are willing to go along with it. Corpsing destroys this suspension of disbelief and turns it back into disbelief again. People can be moved to tears in a theater or in the cinema; real emotions, real sympathies are born from the remembered emotions being portrayed on the stage. Then—one false move, one corpse, and suddenly they are all just actors, pretending. What a let-down.

Corpsing comes from a failure of subjectivity. Suddenly we stop being truthful; we take an objective look from outside our parts, and for a second we are spectators and it's all terribly funny. A second later it's all terribly dead.

A number of people, having just seen a revue or a comedy, ask the actors how it is that they don't laugh at the things which are causing such amusement to the audience. Well, of course, the cast often does find it funny at the read-through, before they have had time to find the truth of their characters. But once that truth has been found and they are playing the real emotion, it is no longer funny to *them*, only to an onlooker. Bewilderment, for instance, is a good source of comedy; being at cross-purposes. But the actors involved are too busy being genuinely bewildered to see the comedy. This is true of real life. You can stand in the street and watch some hilarious things happening, or overhear some priceless conversations on the bus. The participants are absolutely serious, and it is that seriousness that makes it so funny.

Play the truth, believe the truth, and you will be in no danger of corpsing.

Emotional Reverberation

This is a very long label for a very simple concept. Once you have been in the grip of a very strong emotion, that emotion takes quite a while to fade from your behavior and your voice, *even when the reasons for that emotion have been removed or shown to be baseless.* An obvious example is to be found in the phenomenon of shock. If your car overturns, rights itself, and finishes up on the verge, you are going to be very frightened. Now, suppose you examine yourself and find that, miraculously, you are without a scratch or bruise, and then you examine the car and find it perfectly intact, do you immediately return to your former, unruffled state? No. It will take a considerable time for your mind and body to recover.

The same is true of less spectacular cases. If you are very angry at the top of page 56 and the reasons for your anger are effectively demolished by another character, there will still be a kind of backlash of that anger in your next speech, even if it is couched in very reasonable language. You may have had time to regain complete composure by the time you reach page 57, but don't try to lose your anger straightaway just because, on the surface, the words do not imply that it is still there. If you ask somebody to read this line intelligently: "I'm not cross," the chances are that he or she will read it with a half-smile and a lift in intonation at the end of the line, as if it had been preceded by, "What do you mean?" And that's a perfectly intelligent way of interpreting it. But I had precisely that line to deliver in a play while I was still reverberating from anger, and I barked it out—denying its meaning by my intonation: "I'm *not* cross!!!" This is what is called playing against the line: saying one thing, but showing that you mean quite the opposite.

This will happen quite often with emotional reverberation, and it is an interesting way of approaching some lines. "Oh, that is perfectly all right!" "Veronica! How lovely to see you!" "No, really, I love being by myself." "I'm really, really happy!" All those lines can be played straight. They also can be played with emotional reverberation. One could, quite effectively, burst into tears during the last one.

Accent and Inflection

If everything on-stage is significant, then that most certainly includes the voice and the way in which it is used. A voice which can pick up any regional accent it needs to and lose whatever native ones it may have, is obviously the most useful and flexible. Conversely, an accent rooted in a locality that is impossible to shake off is much less adaptable. In an all-Irish production of *Coriolanus* nobody is going to raise a quizzical eyebrow when Coriolanus is played by an Irishman, but within an American cast a strongly-Irish Coriolanus would seem to be saying something. Similarly, it is difficult to imagine Southern accents in Shakespeare, or hard, British accents for the disciples.

There is nothing wrong with a Long Island accent, but just as some parts require that one should not be fat, and some parts require that one should not be thin, some parts will require that one should not have a Long Island accent. Inflection—the vocal shape that one gives to a line—is important, too. If the actor can find the emotional truth behind a line, then the inflection should automatically follow, but it is possible, if you haven't got a good ear, to think the truth but be unable to reproduce it vocally. A monotonous delivery which drops at the end of every sentence and which could be visually reproduced as:

is pretty bad, but it is no worse than the over-bright kind of Playschool delivery where every word is painfully superinflected to the point where it could almost be notated musically. This kind of thing:

This is usually the result of deliberate showing off to the audience and not playing the truth for the other actors. The monotony of the first one is possibly a way of expressing I-feel-like-a-real-idiot.

If you suspect your inflections, or if your best friend mentions it, it might be worth bringing a tape recorder to rehearsal one day so that you can analyze what you are doing when you get home. But do not forget the sanctity of the rehearsal room; this is not for *your* benefit, it is not to keep and threaten the cast with, and it is not for public consumption.

If we learn this much, we will have learned our ABCs. There is no need to be discouraged by that thought; it is no small matter to learn an alphabet. At the same time, the leap from learning an alphabet to creating a book is a big one. The rest of what we need is in ourselves, in our capacity for hard work, frustration, backache, front-ache, eye-ache, and heartache, observation, memory, willpower, intelligence, fitness, determination, and—dare I say it?—talent.

For I do not, I'm afraid, subscribe to the fashionable egalitarian doctrine that anyone can do anything if they are given some instruction. I believe that there are some people who will never make mathematicians, some (like myself) who will never be dancers, some who will never be able to sing, or draw, or learn Chinese, or carve wood, or act without—as my daughter Vicky puts it—turning a drama into a crisis. But that is not to say that people cannot always become better than they are. It is in the nature of things that there is undiscovered talent around in the world, not just theatrical talent, but artistic talent of all varieties. One needs to have a touchstone. If this chapter has been pretty much of a revelation to you and full of ideas that you had not considered up to now, it is, I think, worth asking yourself if you are really cut out to be an actor. If, however, these comments have clarified or captured ideas which you had always felt even at the fringes of your consciousness, then the chances are that you are not going to hit your ceiling of ability for a while.

There are, I am sure, some excellent actors hidden in our congregations; this book has been written in that hope and that belief.

Notes

1. H. Pinter, *The Dumb Waiter*. New York: Grove, 1961.

2. N.F. Simpson, *The Best I Can Do by Way of a Gate-leg Table is a Hundredweight of Coal*. London: Faber & Faber, 1968.

4

The Director

It may be your personal view that two and two make four, but you must not state it in a self-assured way, because this is a democratic country and others may be of a different opinion.

George Mikes, *Down with Everybody*

*G*ood directing is a very specialized skill for which there is really no adequate training ground apart from the theater itself. Even less of the director's art can be taught on paper than the actor's.

The director is responsible for the wholeness of the production: not just for the truth of the performances (his responsibility to the author, which is a primary one), but for the contributions made by the setting, the style, the lighting, the costumes, the music. All these have to be balanced one against another; the director's job is always to bring unity out of diversity, to fasten together what wants to be loose, to channel what will otherwise spill over, to focus and set the blurred and fragmentary.

Analogies always break down beyond a certain point, but it may be helpful to see the director in terms of an orchestral conductor. His responsibility is to allow the audience to hear the symphony. In order to do this he must not only be able to read and understand the score, he must know where the tricky bits are for the players and where they need particular help; he must know where the danger-points are for the shape of the whole piece, where the overall picture may be lost if the dynamics are not carefully controlled; he must have a very good knowledge of the period in which the music was written, as, for instance, in the case of Baroque music, where a composer might employ a sort of shorthand which has to be understood if the work is to sound as it was intended to. He should be able to play one or two orchestral instruments himself and be familiar with the technique of playing others; he should not be repressing his players' abilities or distinctive qualities, but giving them scope. He must have a technique as a conductor, for he is a craftsman in his own right and not just a figurehead. He must have authority and he must be respected and trusted.

I shall not take each of those points and translate it into theatrical terms because it is not really necessary; the rest of the chapter will be an attempt to show how a theater director goes about attaining a similar proficiency. But I will add one more thing: if an ordinary member of the audience were to go away from a concert saying, "What an amazing conductor!" then that conductor would have failed his primary task of revealing the score. Instead, he has put himself and his cleverness up as a barrier between audience and music. What the audience should be saying is, "What an amazing piece of music!"

Of course, there may be professional musicians in the audience who can attain that double-vision of hearing the music afresh and, at the same time, realizing the self-effacing skill and hard work which has gone into achieving such a result. In which case "What an amazing conductor" is a perfectly acceptable response, but there is something wrong if it is the response of the majority of the audience.

"Interpretation" as opposed to "Performance" has become a jargon word in both concert hall and theater. This is what Paul Hindemith has to say on the subject:

The ideal performer will never try to express his own feelings—if ever he thinks that feelings are to be expressed—but the composer's, or whatever he thinks the composer's feelings were. Covering a piece with a thick layer of the performer's so-called feelings means distorting, counterfeiting it. A performer, in doing this, changes his function from that of a transformer to a competing generator—and the shocks received from the clashing of two different currents always hit the innocent listener.[1]

So, let us start out with the idea that the director's primary task is not to use the play he is in charge of to work out his own neuroses or to put a personal gloss on the text, but to convey the truths that the author was concerned to convey. Although I am not fond of using the quotation this way, for it means something entirely different in the context of *Hamlet*, our starting point should be the idea: "The play's the thing."

The Director and Democracy

This chapter opened with a quotation about democracy, an ironic comment which is close to my heart. The word has become less and less a capsule of meaning and more and more a counter in a game of insult and counter-insult.

We should not forget, before we get too worked up about the ideas such a concept arouses in us, that democracy is the name given to a form of government. That is what it is; any other use of the word is no more than metaphorical and must not be taken too literally.

I believe that the wrong understanding of the word "democracy" is what is eating away at the roots of everything which is of greatest value: of art, education, morality, human individuality, talent, and excellence. What has happened is that a stealthy transition has taken place from the truth that we are all of equal value in the sight of God, to the demonstrable untruth that we are all equal.

Are we as tall as one another? As honest as one another? As kind as one another? As musical, as healthy, as intelligent, as reliable as one another? No, of course we are not; we are all at different stages of the journey. We are not all equal in any way except value.

This is what St. Paul expresses in his famous illustration of the body of Christ in 1 Corinthians 12. This is what Menenius Agrippa explains in a very similar way in *Coriolanus*, Act 1, scene i. C.S. Lewis puts it like this:

> No man who says "I'm as good as you" believes it. He would not say it if he did . . . the claim to equality, outside the political field, is made only by those who feel themselves to be in some way inferior . . . "Here is someone who speaks English rather more clearly and euphoniously than I—it must be a vile, upstage, lah-di-dah affectation. Here's a fellow who says he doesn't like hot dogs—thinks he's too good for them, no doubt. Here's a man who hasn't turned on the juke-box—he must be one of those highbrows and is doing it to show off. If they were the right sort of chaps they'd be like me. They've no business to be different; it's undemocratic."
>
> Now this useful phenomenon is by no means new. Under the name of Envy, it has been known to humans for thousands of years. But hitherto they always regarded it as the most odious, and also the most comical of vices . . . The delightful novelty of the present situation is that you can sanction it—make it respectable and even laudable—by the incantatory use of the word *democratic* . . . The basic principle of the new education is to be that dunces and idlers must not be made to feel inferior to intelligent and industrious pupils . . . Children who are fit to proceed to a higher class may be artificially kept back, because

the others would get a *trauma*—Beelzebub, what a useful word!—by being left behind. The bright pupil thus remains democratically fettered to his own age-group throughout his school career, and a boy who would be capable of tackling Aeschylus or Dante sits listening to his coaeval's attempts to spell out A CAT SAT ON THE MAT.[2]

There is a sad, ironic little story of a theater director who worked and worked and worked to form a truly democratic theater company. He finally succeeded; and the company fired him.

Democracy can never be a guiding principle in education or the arts. If the pupil thinks he is as good as the teacher he will never learn anything. If the theater allows the undiscriminating, the untalented, or the inexperienced to have as much sway as the tasteful, the talented, and the wise; if the actor's ideas are as important as the author's; if the unifying vision of the director is allowed to be dissipated by the selfishness of an actor or a lighting designer, then the result is going to be an inchoate mess of private experiences and indulgences.

The director must shoulder his unique responsibility; the other members of the company must trust him to.

But all this is, of course, within the context of something which we said about the conductor: "He should not be repressing his player's abilities or distinctive qualities, but giving them scope." Although we are not allowing this misrepresentation of democracy to interfere with the work, neither are we going to allow the director to be a dictator. He provides the framework of discipline, leadership, criticism, inspiration, and encouragement, but he does this as a *service* to the actors, not as a prop to his self-esteem. Anyone who wishes to be a director in order to implement things is probably in it for the wrong reasons. The director is there to facilitate. He is a coach, not a commander.

The Director's Role

Imagine a group of children making a mural. Each is given a part to be responsible for. Some do shops and houses, some do roads and bridges, some do pedestrians and passers-by, some do cars and trucks. What needs to be done for the whole thing to be assembled properly?

I ask this question because we need to be able to see the connection between the actor's understanding of the "truth" of his part—which I stressed in the chapters on acting and stagecraft—and the director's guidance of the whole. We might ask, for instance, why there is any need for the director at all if *every* member of the cast has really grasped the *truth*. Surely it is bound to work?

Truth, even within the context of one character in a play, is not an absolute concept. If it were, there would only be one possible way of performing *Hamlet* or *A Midsummer Night's Dream*—which is obviously nonsense.

Each child making the mural may have painted his house, or his pedestrian, in a perfectly truthful way, even in an artistically excellent way; and you could still end up with a modern-looking house next to a log cabin, a fourteenth-century peasant driving a herd of cows over a huge suspension bridge toward the Wild West saloon outside which an eighteenth-century fop is arguing with a Victorian lady about where to park his flying saucer. In other words, each child has portrayed what he saw as the truth, and each truth is quite valid in itself, but they don't add up to a homogeneous whole without the help of an overseer who can guide them into working together to produce an artistic unity. The children's creativity will not have been hampered by the limitations put to them—"A modern street," or "An Elizabethan street"—in fact, just the opposite: limitations, even arbitrary ones, are a source of creative energy. This is the kind of energy that the director provokes; in suggesting different approaches, different areas for exploration, in providing a variety of stimuli, he challenges his actors to go beyond their normal areas of thought.

It would not be true to say that actors are lazy—some are—but, as has been pointed out earlier, they do like to be *safe*, and, occasionally, they seek safety in repeating the sort of characterizations they know they can do. The thought is then predigested; all they have to do is polish up on the technical side, get the timing right, make sure of the lines, and—presto—the performance is there. Television and the commercial theater have tended to perpetuate this kind of attitude by casting to type so that the actor plays exactly the same part in a dozen different plays or series. There are actors who have fought successfully against this kind of type-casting, but anyone who has watched murder mysteries, detective shows, or comedies on TV will have seen the same petty thieves, villains, smugglers, secretaries, girlfriends, golden-hearted whores, and down-trodden, overworked desk-sergeants played by the same actors, over and over again. When we categorize characters—Character 36b—it saves rehearsal time, thought, and money, but it's not a lot like acting.

If the rehearsal room itself is a safe place, then the director can push his actors to dare something new; to face new ideas, to try new things, to break through their apparent limitations. But this has to be done in an atmosphere of mutual trust and the seeking of a common good over and above personal gratification.

The Director and his Cast

The relationship between the director and the actors is probably the most important one in the theater. Of course, the director needs a very large amount of factual, technical knowledge about staging, lighting, and movement; he needs to understand, sometimes in the minutest detail, the history and meaning of the text that he and the cast are working on. With some texts he needs to understand the layers of meaning and allusion and symbolism that are present. But a good 50 percent of his work is in the realm of what might be called "Personnel Management." He needs to understand actors, all the different sorts of actors, and how they tick. Some will rely on him for every bit of inspiration and direction he can give; some will resent his interfering in anything they do, and any suggestions or re-directions have to be made with the utmost subtlety. Some will need calming down; some will need stirring up. Some will need to be encouraged to approach their work more intellectually, some will need to be helped away from too much intellectualization and toward more real thought and emotion. Some need encouragement; some need discipline. The list is as endless as the variety of human nature.

One of the difficulties is that actors and directors come at the play from different angles. The director should see the meaning of the whole play, the kind of sweep and force it should have as an entity. The actor, however unselfish he is, will be more concerned with his own contribution to the play. The director starts from the general, the actor from the particular. This is why it is a good idea for both director and cast to refrain from imposing anything on the play in the early stages of rehearsal; fluidity and a willingness to find the answers is better than rigidity and a desire to lay down answers which have to be conformed to.

On the other hand, there are some things which have to be decided before rehearsals start, certain limitations which are creative. The most obvious of these is the set. The designer cannot wait until halfway into rehearsals before he is allowed to get on with the set, so this has to be decided in advance. And this will be the outcome of two different sorts of wisdom—the director's greater understanding of the play and the designer's greater technical expertise. This decision is a kind of reassurance for an actor—a certainty on which he can rely. It gives him the minimum he needs: a definite, physical starting point, an anchor for all his mental explorations. The director will change his mind about such practical matters only at his peril.

By the time the director comes to the first rehearsal, he should have in his mind, or actually on paper, an efficient, sensible, and acceptable blocking for every scene in the play. He should then forget this entirely and inspire the cast to experiment and discover the moves and motives in each scene for themselves. At points of impasse, he can use his own blocking until something better is discovered. Maybe it never will be. In this way the play will grow organically and with the reasoned assent of all the actors—which is always the best and easiest way—but, at the same time, progress will never be held up because of flagging inspiration; there will always be an efficient system of moves ready and waiting in the director's notebook. Apart from anything else, this will inspire trust on the part of the actors in the fact that the director *does* know his stuff and has done his homework. The actors are, after all, in a very vulnerable position and are entitled to look to their director for an answer to any problem. And he should have one. It is up to him, knowing his actors, to decide whether he will give it, or hint at it, or wait until the actor has discovered it himself.

Knowing how actors work will prevent the director from making two mistakes in particular. First, he will not lecture the actors before rehearsals start on meanings, implications, and shapes which *he* has found in the play, but which the actor will not be able to grasp without working toward them from the starting point of his own characterization. The actor may nod and smile at such an academic lecture, but he will not take anything from it because he cannot. Actors just do not work that way without producing uninspired and unsurprising performances.

Second, he will not give direction that the actor is not ready for. Performances are built slowly and carefully, like the pyramids. It is no use waxing eloquent about how the facing-stones of the pyramid are going to be dressed and polished before the foundation blocks have been put into place. At worst it can be detrimental; at best it is a simple waste of time. All new slants, hints, and ideas should be given in order to help the actor progress easily to the next stage of his characterization, not just at random, however true they are.

The director should have the whole of the chapter on stagecraft not just at his fingertips but under his skin, for that chapter was composed with the actor in mind, but the director has to take things one stage further. Not only must he be as single-minded as any of his cast in chasing after the truth and the reality of the characterizations, but he must also have his eye on the whole canvas—the balancing of scene against scene, the smaller climaxes placed perfectly within the larger ones, the overall onward movement, the changes of pace, the beauty, the shape, the cadences of the whole play. But, in order to get an actor to fit into this large picture, direction must be given in terms of his immediate motivation, not in terms of the whole. Let me give a concrete example. If, for instance, the director feels that, for the benefit of the whole play, Scene 10 should be played at a much quieter level, he must not put it to the actor in such a way. As far as his personal motivation is concerned, it will not make sense. He needs a definite, concrete reason for playing the scene quietly, not just a vague generalization, so you have to give him a direction of this sort: "I think at this stage Arnold is so bored with the whole argument that he answers rather casually, even listlessly to everything Anna says." Or even better would be, "Don't forget that her mother is asleep in the room above; you'll have to keep your voices down, or she'll be downstairs before the kettle's even boiled." This gives a whole new and positive dimension to the actor. It has creative possibilities, tension, a kind of excitement. Merely to say, "I don't want that scene too loud" is a very wishy-washy and negative comment. It comes under the heading of "Forgettable Direction," and as such should be avoided. Positive direction is always easier to accept, understand, and play.

Charles Marowitz, in *The Act of Being*, draws up a list of opposing attitudes held by different sorts of actors which he designates "Trads" and "Mods." While restraining myself from making any moral judgment on the rightness of any of these views, it is worth reproducing the list to show prospective directors the different sorts of demands which they are going to have to answer in their directing style. Any cast is liable to contain actors on both sides of the list—sometimes on both sides at once!—and you should know how you will answer or accommodate such demands.

Let's get it blocked	Let's get it analyzed
Fix inflections and "readings"	Play for sense and let inflections take care of themselves
Block as soon as possible	Move freely for as long as possible
Play for laughs	Play for contact
Final decisions as soon as possible	Final decisions as late as possible and always open to reversal
It was a bad house	It was a bad performance
I take orders	I give suggestions
Am I being masked?	Am I important at this moment in the play?

Can I be heard?	Are my intentions clear?
I'm getting nothing from my partner	I'm not getting what I expected so I shall adjust
Just as we rehearsed it	As the immediacy of the performance dictates
Let's get on with it and stop intellectualizing	Let's apply what reason we have to the problem at hand
More feeling	More clarity of intention so as to produce more feeling
Hold that pause	Fill that pause
Everything's in the lines	Everything's in the sub-text
I'll play this role symbolically	I can't play concepts, only actions
I am the villain	I refuse to pass moral judgments on my character
My many years of professional experience convince me that . . . [3]	Nothing is ever the same

The Director at Rehearsal

Though an experienced director will, through trial and error—or, if he is very lucky, through trial and success—have worked out what is for him the best method of approaching a new cast and a new text, it is useful for the beginner to have some sort of overall scheme which he can use as a starting point and which he can discard or depart from when it is no longer useful or when he has discovered a personal and more efficient way.

It is worth pointing out, though, that the following schedule is not mere theory; it is based on standard practice mixed with a little personal taste. Thus, if it has not the force of divine commandment, it has the practical guarantee of discovered truth.

Before the first rehearsal is called, the director will have read the play several times and be familiar with its shape, structure climaxes, characters, problem areas, and so forth. He will understand the meaning of the text and any layers of allusion or allegory or other devices which it employs. He and the designer will have discussed the design and, if appropriate, a scale model of the finished set will be available for the actors to see. He will have decided on any additional material necessary—choreography, music, stage-fighting, or special movement—and made appropriate arrangements for their coaching and incorporation. He will have read any other texts or books which throw light on the play or upon the theme and perhaps have revised his knowledge of any other works by the playwright he is dealing with. He will have made arrangements with the stage manager to set about making or finding any particularly difficult or complicated props. He will have discussed the costume design with the designer, and these, too, should be available for the cast to look at. Most fundamental of all, he will have made sure that a rehearsal space has been secured and that an adequate number of scripts is available.

The first rehearsal will be used for one or two read-throughs during which the cast can get to know one another, the play, and the director.

Though the atmosphere should be as relaxed and as free as possible from tension, the read-through must be taken seriously or one of the most important moments in the rehearsal time will be wasted. For it is at this point alone that the cast can take in the play not just as actors but as audience as well. Unless the play is extremely well-known, this is the only opportunity for genuine surprise and spontaneity; the plot, the characters, the dialogue all unfold for the first time. It is not too absurd to suggest that, in some cases, the majority of the rehearsal period is taken up with the attempt to regain the freshness of the first read-through.

For the director, this first reading will provide an insight into the instinctive reaction of the characters to one another. Even at this stage, a chance inflection or a particular exchange between two of the actors may give him a sudden illumination or a clue to the way to play a particular scene. It may, on the other hand, prove to him that one of the ideas he has had is *not* going to work in the way he had thought. All knowledge, at this stage, is progress.

If there is a good deal of time left after the read-through, it could be used in working at one of the important scenes of the play—trying some experiments with it, pulling it to pieces, building it up. Remember that it is not necessary to work through the scenes chronologically; there may be one scene which holds the key to a character. If so, for the actor's sake, that must be worked on first so that the others can follow logically.

At such an early stage in rehearsal, both director and actors will want to be roughing in the outlines, rather as a painter does, before starting work in great detail. The picture must be built up slowly and logically. This will often, but not necessarily always, mean working through from the beginning to end during the early days.

On the first day of full rehearsal, the floor should be marked up by the stage manager. This simply means indicating, with chalk or, preferably, tape, the positioning of the set: where the steps start and finish, where the doors are, where the ramp starts and so on. If this is not done accurately, there will be such a huge difference when the time comes to work with the set itself, that the whole play will begin to wilt. Sometimes there is not enough room for the business that has been rehearsed, sometimes distances are too great and moves have to be changed. Steps are suddenly much lower or much higher than the cast had imagined, or doors open inward not outward. All these tiny details add up to a positive migraine for the actors who already have a brainful of ideas, emotions, and problems to cope with.

Quite often the cast do not find themselves on the set, wearing the right costumes, using the right props, in the right degree of light or darkness until the last two rehearsals. No wonder the first night is thought of as such an ordeal. Proper marking up can help avoid the worst traumas, but there is *no* substitute for using the real thing—whether it is a whole set, a dribbling teapot, a heavy sword, or a floor-length cloak—just as soon as possible.

After a day or two, the director will want to start working in more depth on certain scenes. This will not involve the whole cast. He should make a schedule of calls a day or two in advance so that the actors will know between what hours they are needed and can spend the rest of the time studying their parts. There is nothing so frustrating to an actor who has a lot to do, as to spend a whole day waiting around to work and then going home without having done anything. It is draining on both energy and commitment. The stage manager is responsible for making sure that everything the director needs, from a microphone to a pack of cards, to an actor, is there for him when he wants it.

Actors, on the whole, are the ones who are going to want to carry on working in detail on individual scenes—making sure everything is working for them, making sure they know exactly what is going on, crafting, polishing, digging, looking for new details, and making the most of their moments. The director, since he continually has the needs of the whole play in his mind, is the one who will want to see how the entire piece hangs together.

There is no way of explaining how to judge when the time is ripe for the first run-through, but it is a fair bet to say that it will be slightly later than the director would like and slightly earlier than the cast would like.

The director should realize that, when it comes, it is going to be a terrible anticlimax for the actors. Having only had to keep the sense of a single scene, or maybe two, in their heads up to this point, the suddenness with which certain points arrive, or the unexpected jolts that occur when scenes are linked together for the first time, can disorient the cast and can result in carefully worked scenes suddenly reverting to chaos.

This is only a temporary state of affairs and is due not to a sudden failure of acting ability, but to a failure of concentration leading to a loss of nerve. The result will be a depressed and distressed cast.

This will not matter a bit, *so long as the director is pleased* and can shrug off the minor disasters which he foresaw and be encouraging about the shape and pace of the whole thing. Indeed, a temporarily distressed cast is a cast which is going to leap wholeheartedly into trying to remove the reasons for that depression and work much harder in the ensuing days.

If, however, the director has not foreseen what is going to happen and is himself surprised and disappointed, the cast will lose their faith in him and in themselves, and it will take a super-human effort to lift them off the floor onto their feet again.

So, it's back to the drawing-board again for a day or so; and then another run. The first two or three runs should be interruptible if the cast or the director want to stop and put things right; but, as the end of the rehearsal period approaches, and detailed rehearsal is still being done, the runs should be done "for real" without stopping, no matter what goes wrong. After a run has finished, the director will gather the cast round a cup of coffee and give notes. During the run, he will have written down, or dictated to his stage manager so that he himself need never remove his eyes from the stage, notes on the performance—tiny changes, incorporations of things that happen by accident, adjustments here, refinements there. These he then communicates to the actors, concentrating wherever possible on causes rather than symptoms when things have gone wrong, and mingling in plenty of praise and encouragement.

These note sessions, where the whole company joins in an analysis and discussion of its work, can be times of great delight and communion. It is probably better, if serious criticism or even rebuke is to be given, that it should be done alone with the individual involved. It is tactless and unfair to single out an actor, however difficult he has been. Note sessions are serious but not solemn times, and an actor should not feel isolated from the company by heavy words from the director; it will only do harm to the general atmosphere and be counter-productive for a long time, if not for the duration.

The director should always remember that he is there to provide an atmosphere in which hard work is enjoyable and creativity can flourish. Discipline should not be a problem so long as the director can show, through his work, that he is worthy of respect, and so long as he does not enjoy his position solely for the sense of power it gives him. People must be taught to respect the work of others by being quiet during work and by arriving on time; after that, the group will, ideally, discipline itself. One cannot really legislate for a group of actors who do not really want to act.

The Later Stages of Rehearsal

Once the play has reached a state where runs are possible, it is time to bring in the lighting designer so that he can see the lighting requirements—the areas to be lit, the atmosphere of each scene, the special lights for particular effects and the way the scenes flow into one another or, alternatively, snap from one to another.

The first couple of runs will be for this kind of purpose: to remind the cast of the shape, length, and climaxes of the whole, and to demonstrate this to the technical staff who provide the conditions under which it can best be performed.

It is, however, quite a good idea to keep the cast fresh, thoughtful, and open to the possibility of new ideas by doing a run for a particular purpose, perhaps to the exclusion of other purposes. For instance, it can be a good idea to do a run simply for pace; characterization, motivation, etc. are flung aside and the cast concentrates entirely at keeping the play going at a speedy pace, picking up cues fast, entering without a split-second's pause on someone else's exit, and so forth.

Runs can also be done on the following premises:

1. Imagine you are making the play up as you go along.

2. Do it all with strong British, Southern, or New York accents.

3. Sing it all, as if it were an opera, in any style you like.

4. Imagine you are all wearing suits of armor/wanting desperately to be anywhere other than where you are/convinced that every other character on the stage is a spy.

Admittedly these all sound rather silly, and you may not get through more than a third of the play with some—notably the third. But it is surprising how these exercises will lift the spirits of a jaded cast, and how many insights and surprises will follow such experiments.

The climax of rehearsals, even though it is seldom an emotional climax for the actors, is when everything at last comes together for the dress rehearsal and the technical rehearsal.

A dress rehearsal is exactly what its name implies: a run of the play from start to finish with everybody in full costume.

A technical rehearsal is for the benefit of both actors and technicians. It means rehearsing, and getting right, every effect, every lighting change, every sound effect, every set-change, every entrance and exit, every practical prop (that is, a prop such as a cigarette lighter or a bottle full of sherry or a candle or a balloon, that actually has to be used) as well as all the explosions, poltergeists, window-breakings, and secret-panel workings that the script might demand. This need not be done in costume unless a costume change has to be timed to see how possible it is, or unless the lighting designer wants to see the effect of his lights on a particular costume, whether a character is going to be seen in the blackout and so forth.

This is the most arduous time for everyone involved, not least the director, and it is here that the concentration and the patience of the company is going to be severely tested. I have attended technicals that lasted from two in the afternoon until four in the morning, and one that was still only half-finished as the audience for the first performance was coming in on the other side of the curtains.

Since these are the final chances (and sometimes the *first* chances) to get everything absolutely right, on the set with all the technical back-up, it is not so much a wonder that they last so long, but that they can ever be shorter.

The director must make his choice of how to run these final rehearsals, depending on the state of the play and the readiness of the technical facilities.

A fairly usual scheme is to have, first, a full dress rehearsal for the actors. Costume problems will then be able to be solved. This should be a run during which the actors or the director can call a halt any time in order to get things right. Then a technical rehearsal, as has been described above; and finally, a full technical dress rehearsal in which everything takes place just as at a performance and nobody stops for any reason.

If the actors have been allowed a proper dress rehearsal, the technical rehearsal can be topped and tailed. This means getting one technical thing right and then, leaving out as much play as is necessary, skipping to the next light cue or effect, getting that one right—however many times it takes—and skipping to the next one, and so on.

It is a wearisome, dispiriting but entirely necessary process, during which the director will probably have to make as many vitally important decisions as he has made over the entire rehearsal period, at the same time as trying to keep everybody optimistic and good-humored.

The Director and the Performance

In the professional theater, where a production will never run for less than three weeks and can run for three years, there is often an important role for the director to play once the show is under way. Even the very best of amateurs, however, seldom have such luxury. If the play is a one-time in the local theater or school hall, there is little a director can do if he is not fully satisfied with the end product, except to keep that knowledge under his belt and to learn from the experiences, both good and bad. Every production should be a step forward, a growth, for everyone involved.

If, as is quite likely, there are two or three performances, then the director's work may not be over when the first night arrives. But he must know what he is about.

There is a sense in which the work should be finished by the time the first night comes. There has been a rehearsal period, decisions have been taken, now comes the result. Full stop. It is too late to have second thoughts, too late to make changes.

If the show seems to have gone down well, this is certainly how the cast are liable to feel. They will probably resent any further intrusion on the part of the director. But what if the director can see glaring errors? Things going wrong? Parts that could easily be tidied up? Is it wrong for him to try to do this before the second performance?

I do not think it is—provided he is dealing with details and provided he is not just being over-fussy. No actor will mind being given a few notes in the light of a first performance with an audience. No actor will mind a director saying, "You were right about that move in Act 2; it doesn't work—go back to what you suggested," and if the cast and the director are both working sensibly together for the good of the play, it is likely that the notes he gives will already have been felt, even subconsciously, by the actors. It is, however, much too late to change the concept of the production, the characterizations, and the overall shape. Notes should be kept to those aspects of the production that can be improved in an hour or so. One would expect them to be about the odd move, about pace generally or in particular, about diction or pauses or talking during a laugh, or a piece of business which is not quite slick enough, and about technical matters.

What the director must resist is discouragement. A first night is an ordeal for an actor, and when it is over he is entitled to the relief and delight he will feel even if he is very self-critical. So, before the first performance, the director should limit himself to encouraging the cast, wishing them luck, and—if he has to—limiting himself to only one or two small reminders to each actor about his performance.

After the first night he should say nothing that is not encouragement or praise and give a call for notes for the next day before the performance. Notes given after—or even, heaven forbid, during—a performance are terribly depressing, counter-productive, and will almost certainly be forgotten, or worse, deliberately ignored. By the time the next performance arrives, everyone will be in a much more receptive mood and will be wanting to know what the director *really* thought. This description of how the great Russian violinist David Oistrakh criticized his pupils is a revealing one:

The student played the whole sonata to its end, David listened with the greatest attention. When she had finished, he said: "Great, wonderful, you are making tremendous progress. You improved the intonation, enriched the dynamics, and the chords don't sound so dull as before, etc." (sic)

The joy visible on the girl's face increased with each minute. Because the very flattering comments lasted for quite a long time her happiness grew immensely. As soon as the girl felt she was a true violinist, David began to criticize:

"I have discovered a few weaknesses," and he then proceeded to analyze the sonata bar by bar.

He talked about the style, phrasing, rhythm, and demonstrated after each remark how to eliminate mistakes of which there were thousands.

The violinist followed every word intently, but her happy mood didn't leave her as the master's tone didn't lose any of its warmth in spite of the substantial corrections. You got the feeling that the challenge to overcome these "unimportant" mistakes would not only give the violinist the greatest satisfaction but it would also increase her faith in her own ability.[4]

This technique is well worth copying by any director. I call it a technique, and yet for anyone who considers the worth of other people before anything else, it is mere courtesy.

What is most interesting about working in the theater, in whatever capacity, is that you soon discover that it is best done by truly loving your neighbor as yourself; by determining the success of the play or of other people before your own success, you thereby determine and secure that as well.

Notes

1. P. Hindemith, *A Composer's World*. Cambridge, Mass.: Harvard University Press, 1952.

2. C.S. Lewis, *Screwtape Proposes a Toast*. New York: Macmillan, 1967.

3, C. Marowitz, *The Act of Being*. North Pomfret, Vt.: Secker and Warburg, 1978.

4. Jusefovich, *David Oistrakh*. Cassell, 1979.

5

Church and Theater

If you can keep your head when all about you are losing theirs, it's just possible you haven't grasped the situation.
Jean Kerr, *Please Don't Eat the Daisies*

*E*verything that I have said so far about acting and thinking applies just as much to sketches as to plays; in order to act convincingly for three minutes, it is necessary to use the same approach and technique as you would if you were acting for three hours. For the director, too, there is no difference in the qualities he needs to bring to directing a sketch from those he will employ on a full-length production. It is in conception and writing that the sketch differs from the play, and we shall be looking at the writing and constructing of sketches in the next chapters.

There will, however, be many people who are seeking advice not only on the techniques of their art, but on the allied subjects of integrating it into the context of a church service or a worship meeting, teaching and educating without offending, allaying the suspicions of an audience which is not theatrically educated, or even trying to satisfy the pastor and keep their own integrity. This

short chapter will look at one or two such problems and see if the
beginnings of a solution can be found.

The Church as Theater

The church makes a very bad theater. A theater is designed to focus
the attention on the areas where it should be focused; it does this
through the provision of seats which always face the right way
(which they don't, always, in a church), through the provision of a
complete and perfect blackout (which is seldom to be found in the
most modern of churches), through lighting (and which church can
be adequately lit for theater without days of work?), through
acoustics which allow the actors to be heard in every part of the
auditorium (which is not traditionally a feature of church buildings), and through the attention expected of an audience (which is
a different kind of attention from that expected of a congregation).

A company of actors must, therefore, ask itself the basic question, "Is the church the very best place to perform?" and if—taking
all these things into consideration—the answer is still "Yes," they
must set about adapting either the building or their material for
such a performance.

Audibility and visibility are the two primary requisites for a
theatrical performance. If the seats of the church are not raked, then
some sort of stage is going to be necessary. The penalties for not
using a stage will be that the actors will be visible only from about
the shoulders upward to all except the front two or three rows; they
will disappear from sight if they ever sit down; and kneeling, lying,
or crawling are completely out of the question. This may all seem
very obvious, but it can come as a terrible shock, after rehearsing
in the wide open spaces of the church hall, to bring your offering
into the family service and find, suddenly, that only about thirty
people will know that it has even happened.

It is possible to do without a stage if the church can be emptied
of seats and the congregation is willing to sit around you on the

floor, but it is very doubtful whether this could ever be done during a service.

Lighting may not be too much of a problem. Assuming that the actors are not actually hidden, there should be enough light in the church for them to be seen. But everything else in the church will be just as clearly seen as well, and the background of organ-pipes, singing group, flowers, and stained glass is not conducive to concentration. If you turn off all the lights except those above the acting area, you get strange shadows on their faces and a generally washed-out atmosphere. Bring in some lights on stands, and you start masking off parts of the acting area from some of the congregation.

A solution can only be found in individual cases. No theoretical solution will fit every church building. But a sensible basis for starting would be to bring in extra lighting if it can be set up in front of pillars and thus not obstruct the vision any more than usual; have a set of flats or screens painted in a darkish color and set them up as backdrop for the action to block off distracting clutter or decoration. This will have the added advantage of providing easy exits and entrances.

Acoustics are slightly more difficult. While it is true that a properly trained voice will be able to cope with most buildings of parish church size, it is still not an easy task, and any cough or clatter from those watching is magnified by a church acoustic to destructive proportions. If someone drops a Bible a whole line can be lost, and Forde's Law dictates that any such disturbance *always* happens on key lines. In addition to this, most churches—quite often unnecessarily—employ a PA system. This means that the congregation can hear without any effort at all. After such luxury the ear does not easily adjust to listening to unamplified voices; even if the actors *can* actually be heard, the sudden lack of amplification will make the audience *think* that they cannot hear.

Actors, of course, cannot use a PA unless they are totally static, or unless it is a very sophisticated system with hanging or cordless microphones that are not too directional. Normally, however, there are two or three stand microphones, and that's it.

A distinction must be drawn between a theatrical performance in a church and a performance within the context of a service. In the case of the former the acoustic problem may not arise since the ear will adjust to the level of the actors' voices without having been lulled by the amplified voice beforehand. In the latter case one either ignores the problem and hopes for the best or chooses material which is narrated rather than acted.

The Context of Worship

In the field of linguistics there is a term which is known as "register." It applies to the different kinds of language which we use for different contexts. It is nothing to do with dialect or putting on a posh voice; it is nothing to do with cheating or pretending. It is something to do with appropriateness and tact.

A nuclear physicist will not employ the same register in talking to his wife and family as that which he uses when talking to his colleagues at work. A schoolboy will speak in one register on the playground and in another in the classroom. The register which I am using in order to write this book is subtly different from the one I would use if I were lecturing to you in a seminar and very different from that which I would use if I were discussing exactly the same problems with you over a cup of coffee.

A similar kind of register applies to the use of theatrical material. I have, for instance, written a sketch about covetousness which, although it makes points very strongly and is written from a very positive Christian understanding of the matter, is not one which it would be advisable to perform in a church. The theme is fine; the register is wrong.

When writing or choosing material for a church service, it is important to keep this concept of register firmly in mind. It is not simply a matter of honesty or dishonesty, it is just a matter of what is acceptable in a certain context. The nuclear physicist's wife will surely not object to her husband's cold, exact, technical jargon in context, but she might not have said "Yes" if he had proposed to her in terms of the integration of compatible bio-systems.

Let us take a look at the four main areas in which theater can be used in a church service. I have identified these as:

1. Prophetic
2. Evangelistic
3. Didactic
4. Entertaining

Each of these categories needs to be combined with the fourth in order to make a successful sketch; the fourth category is the only one which can stand on its own, but probably won't if it is to work properly in church. Most sketches are a combination of all four categories.

Prophetic theater is theater which clarifies the Word of God at a particular time. *Evangelistic* theater is that which clarifies the gospel in particular. *Didactic* theater—in this context—clarifies the teaching of the Bible. And *Entertaining* theater is based on the nature of humankind and creation.

I have not included in this list the idea of theater as worship because I find that a very difficult concept. Theater can certainly be worship, a spiritual sacrifice, on the part of the actor; theater may result in the congregation being able to worship more fully, but only because it has taught them something, reminded them of something, or prophesied to them—not because it has, in itself, been a worshipful experience. Theater does not work like that. Even a short sketch has to be attended to in a unique way if it is to work. The abstractions of music and dance have their own logic, and it is a real one, but it is not the logic of words and theater. Theater has to be followed and understood if it is to say anything. Music, dance, praise, and prayer are all tending to reconciliation:

theater thrives on conflict. Worship is concerned with reality; theater is always a step away from reality. Theater must be true, but it cannot be more than a metaphor for the truth that worship deals with.

It is for this reason that I believe it is sensible to place any sketch performed in church during the ministry of the Word, instead of a reading, for instance, or during a sermon. It is at such points that the congregation is expecting teaching or exhortation; they are prepared to listen.

"Involvement" is another of those words that is bandied around with as much, or as little, intelligence as "relevance." Involvement is a blanket term for many different sorts of activity. I am involved in politics, I am involved in theater, I am involved with my family, but not at all in the same ways and not with the same sort of commitment. Yes, of course good theater does involve the audience, but it is qualitatively different from the involvement that worship demands.

The World, the Flesh, and the Pastor

This is perhaps the most difficult relationship to get right. The congregation may take to a sketch in the service as a duck takes to water. On the other hand there is no reason why they should. The church as a body of people has not been famed for its easy acceptance of new ideas and methods. Nor have Christians as a body been famed for their excellence in the theatrical arts. Is there a *need* for the use of drama in your church? Who says? Can you provide it with at least the same degree of excellence as the pastor provides teaching and the musicians provide music?

The point is that the introduction—or even the continuance—of a dramatic element in the service should not be a three-way fight between the world (the congregation), the flesh (you), and the pastor. Theater in church will not survive if the pastor does not approve and, more, does not know how to use it to the best advantage. It cannot survive if the world doesn't want it. And, whether it survives or not, it won't make a bit of difference to anybody if God doesn't want it.

A sketch is no good if it merely interrupts a sermon; it is no good if it merely performs badly something which the pastor could do much better with a story or a joke; it's no good if it makes the pastor look incompetent.

Integration is absolutely necessary. The pastor must be allowed to see a script of the sketch before he has written his sermon. It would be a good idea if he could see a fairly polished rehearsal too, for reading a script is an acquired skill, and he may not realize quite how much it says or quite how memorably it says it. He can then let the sketch speak for itself rather than re-echo a point he has already made. He can use the sketch and the characters to talk about in his sermon. He can build up to the sketch so that it does a good deal of his work for him; a sketch used in this way can even stop before it reaches a conclusion (some logical conclusions are too "pat" for theater) and let the pastor continue. A sketch can, perhaps, put one point of view, and the pastor can then demolish it. It is, for instance, very easy to show family life—to take an obvious example—at its very worst; theater thrives on that sort of conflict. It is ineffably hard to show the other side of the coin—a family in perfect harmony. But if the pastor can pick up properly after the sketch, the conflict will probably be enough. Sometimes pastors have to be taught a bit. He may not realize, when he asks for one, that a sketch showing any relationship working perfectly is an impossible task for theater. Actors and pastors can learn together.

I had the experience, many times, of working with David Watson, the best-known clergyman in England, and never ceased to marvel at the way in which he made our sketches into an integral part of his talk. He knew just when to break off, just how to pick up on themes and ideas. We, in our turn, learned just how to write sketches that would complement his teaching. He built the house;

we put in the windows. They probably rattled a bit when we first started, but in an atmosphere of mutual trust and respect "interpreted by love," we found a way.

It is not the same way for everybody; every circumstance is different. This is why I am wary of laying down principles other than to remember that whether you are a church leader, an actor, a writer, or a critical member of the congregation, you are all there to serve one another and not to do your own thing. If you believe that theater in church is wrong, be prepared to give it a chance and change your mind. If you believe that it is right, be prepared to give way to other people's tastes and desires.

In the end, the best place to perform, for virtually every reason, is somewhere other than a church. You won't have to fit in with people's preconceptions of what ought to happen; you won't have to worry about the sanctity of your surroundings; you won't have to cope with church architecture or acoustics. Apart from anything else, you'll have a chance of preaching to people other than the converted.

Street Theater

Street theater bears about the same relation to real theater as kicking a dustbin does to symphonic music. Street theater has to be loud, bright, and captivating. The best street theater is the result of deep thought, hard work, and a brilliant concept. It is an art that can work like magic, but it is a specialized art. It is not indoor theater taken outside and shouted with a silly hat on. I know little about real street theater and have seen scarcely any. I have seen a great deal of substandard ranting in silly clothes which has been called street theater, but that is not what this book is about, and if you want advice on outdoor performances you must find yourself an expert, for I am not.

6

Writing

True ease in writing comes from art, not chance,
As those move easiest who have learn'd to dance.
Alexander Pope, *An Essay on Criticism*

*A*nd that's true enough, though it doesn't get us very far. We do not need to be told that art produces the best writing; what we need is some indication of how that art might be attained. Even the idea of attaining to art—even to efficiency—is a novelty for some people. When I am asked where I get my ideas from, I know, first of all, that the questioner has never written anything himself, or he would not ask such a ridiculous question. Secondly, I know that an honest answer is going to disappoint him or her. Somehow it always does. What such people want, if they are honest, is a magical solution.

If I were to say, "What you do is go into a stationer's and buy a small, brown notebook, four and a half inches by seven inches. You don't open it. You take it home, place it on your desk, pray for at least five minutes, dedicating the book to God, and then, when you open it, ideas will flood from your brain onto the blank pages; ideas of the subtlest, most contagious and original kind, ideas which will be the envy of every preacher and a powerful weapon in the spiritual battles of the twentieth century," that would be perfectly acceptable.

If they are not quite naive enough to believe this, they will certainly believe that once they have decided to be writers they will become the possessors of an equivalent of the carpenter's toolbox or the plumber's carpetbag of tricks.

And that really is the key: "a bag of tricks." A blueprint, a method, an infallible way is what people search for. So I had better say at the outset that I can supply nothing of the kind. Art may create magic, but magic will never create art. In every fairy story and every myth it is always the one who tries the selfish shortcut who gets hammered. The third son—for it is usually the third son—works hard, toils, journeys, uses his imagination. It is only when he has done that that he receives any supernatural help he is going to get.

If you have to think of yourself in some terms other than merely a writer, better far to choose the miller's son than the prince. At the same time, however, one should not be prevented by a false sense of modesty from choosing the very best models to learn from. A genius will, in the end, overtake and overshadow all those whom he has taken as his teachers; most of us, though, must be content to approach our models and so it is foolish to choose anything less than the best. And I think one must go about deciding who is the best in a pragmatic kind of way—the best for one purpose will not necessarily be the best for another.

What I am not suggesting—and I had better make this clear now—is simple, straightforward copying of somebody else's style or ideas. What a waste of time to reproduce what has already been achieved, and worse still to reduce a whole symphony of sound, color, and texture to a single finger dabbing at a broken-winded harmonium.

But it should not surprise us that the best way of discovering how a thing is done is to look at examples of how others have done it. This is the very essence of study in any field, literary or scientific.

A knowledge of what has already been discovered gives us a map for our own future explorations. We can delve deeper into some of the caves marked upon it, we can cut out a deeper channel for one of its rivers or build a bridge over it, we can even go off the map altogether if that is what excites us, but it would be foolish to ignore the map completely.

To change the analogy, I suppose it is conceivable that someone, never having sat in a car in his life except as a passenger, could leap into the driver's seat and go forty miles without injury to himself or to anybody else. But if he really wants to be Al Unser or Mario Andretti he would do well to be taught from the outset by someone who can drive and, even better, to know something of what goes on under the hood.

All this need hardly have been said a century ago, but today writers and readers seem to put quite an unwonted premium on originality as distinct from any other literary quality. What is important is not so much originality, which can be either exhilarating or confusing depending on your point of view, as authenticity. If something is authentic, true, it is worth having done it, but the fact that it has never been done before (unless it is authentic as well) does not prove that it ought to have been done at all.

The ancient writers saw things in a very different way from us. As C.S. Lewis has pointed out:

> I doubt if they would have understood our demand for originality or valued those works in their own age which were original any the more on that account. If you had asked Layamon or Chaucer "Why do you not make up a brand new story of your own?" I think they might have replied (in effect), "Surely we are not yet reduced to that?"[1]

In a much later century Samuel Johnson says of Pope: "He saw immediately . . . in the works of others, what was to be shunned, and what was to be copied." And, lest we think Pope himself would have objected to being exposed thus, here is what he says himself: "My first taking to imitating was not out of vanity, but humility. I saw how defective my own things were, and endeavored to mend my manner by copying good strokes from others."

Roger Ascham, the most famous of Elizabethan teachers, taught that imitation of the ancients was the best way to learn how to write. Shakespeare himself was a jobbing playwright and knew very well his debt to other poets and dramatists. Every major writer, even of our own century, has acknowledged influences, writers whose work has been a sudden revelation or inspiration.

It seems, then, that the primary requisite for being a good writer is to be, first of all, a good reader. Studying the map, if you like—looking under the hood.

A writer's reading should be broad and not restricted to the genre in which he is going to specialize. A man might say, for instance, that he wished to be a composer of simple, short choral pieces. But there would be something suspicious about him if he were not already acquainted with a great deal of different sorts of music, if he had never been attracted by lieder, opera, concertos, cantatas, chamber music, or symphonies. If he had learned nothing from, or found nothing to admire in the medieval, the baroque, classical, romantic, nationalistic, or contemporary styles in all their diversity. If all he had heard were short, simple choral pieces before setting out to write more of the same, it could almost be predicted that they would be dull, superficial, and ephemeral.

The same is true for writers. Every author can teach us something worth learning, even if it is in a negative sense—the path not to take. So, however much you have read before, read more. Do not despise—embrace. Do not sip—devour. Do not prejudge—experience. A man writes not from poverty but from riches. If you have only a few scattered pennies at the bottom of your purse, what can you hope to spend on your audience? Or are you determined on cheapness because hard work is too much of an expense?

Let's go back for a moment to that questioner we met at the beginning of this chapter. He wanted to know where ideas came from (that is, he wonders why he never has any himself and wants to know the secret). A conversation with him might go something like this:

Questioner:	I wish I could get ideas like you do.
Writer:	Well, Montaigne might have said that he didn't have any ideas, whereas . . .
Questioner:	Montaigne?
Writer:	Well . . . Lamb, then. It's interesting how ideas seem to come . . .
Questioner:	I haven't read any Lamb.
Writer:	No? Well . . . he probably isn't very fashionable these days. But if you study almost any poem from Herrick to Geoffrey Hill . . .
Questioner:	I don't read poetry.
Writer:	Not even Shakespeare?
Questioner:	We did one in school.
Writer:	Which one was that?
Questioner:	The one about that king.
	(*Pause*)
Writer:	Oh . . . yes . . . er, *that* one. Well, leave Shakespeare for a minute. If you think of the novels that you have read, even a single idea in Jane Austen, for instance . . .
Questioner:	We didn't do her.
Writer:	Pardon me?
Questioner:	At school. We didn't do her.
Writer:	So you haven't read any?
Questioner:	Not Jane Austen, no.
Writer:	Nor George Eliot?
Questioner:	Didn't do him either.

Writer:	Charles Williams?
Questioner:	No.
Writer:	Max Frisch?
Questioner:	No.
Writer:	Robert Graves?
Questioner:	No.
Writer:	William Golding?
Questioner:	Er . . .
Writer:	Yes?
Questioner:	No.
Writer:	But you have read a novel?
Questioner:	Oh, yes!
Writer:	What was it, then?
Questioner:	Um . . . rats! . . . Now you're asking! . . . It was a green one . . .
Writer:	Do you read the newspapers? Go to art galleries? Listen to the radio? Do you read biographies? Autobiographies? Go to concerts? Read your children stories? Nursery rhymes? Do any of your jelly jars have labels that you have looked at? . . .

There is probably no need to go any further. The end of the scenario reveals that the questioner is a Christian, reads devotional books and testimonies, reads his Bible assiduously and goes to church meetings, and believes that the Lord is telling him to become a Christian writer.

How can you write a play if you've never read one? Or if you have read only two? Or three. Or four. How many do you have to read? As many as it takes. Our imaginary questioner can never become a writer because he does not know what a writer is or what a writer does. He may be an honest, sincere, and wise man; one can be wise by a gift of God, but one can expound that wisdom on the stage only by a long, indeed never-ending, apprenticeship.

Writers are, on the spiritual and mental plane, as important as surgeons are on the physical. Constantly we are being told, quite truthfully, that we are what we eat. But man does not live by bread alone. We are, just as surely, what we read and what we hear. If our mental attitudes, as many doctors are asserting, can be linked with cancers in the body, how much more can they be linked with cancers in the soul? To be a writer—even one attended to by a small, local fellowship—is a tremendous privilege and a fearful responsibility.

But to practice an art a man must be interested in that art and not just in the (unforeseeable) results that his work will have on an audience. And the reason that the most trenchant, memorable, and truthful statements about ourselves and the universe come from outside the Christian church is that Christians are all too easily shocked by reality; they want the truth to be completely beautiful. Whereas the real truth about truth in a fallen world is that it is likely to be both beautiful and horrible, both pure and filthy.

It may be true that the world has tended to concentrate on the "crucifixion" aspect of the truth—the dirt, the pain, the waste, even the absurdity. But is it not equally true that the church has tended to ignore the "crucifixion" and to concentrate on the "resurrection" aspect of truth? Both falsify, but the world's view is more likely to carry weight because it is truer to normal experience. Only the Christian artist can balance the two, for he is the one who can understand both, who can, with his foot in both camps, be the go-between.

It is not an easy or enviable job, but it is Christlike; to bring what one has been given of the divine into the dungheap, to refuse to shut one's eyes to both beauty and the beast.

What the Christian has to understand is how to communicate with the world, for one part of it—"the secular"—would have him compromise his message and concentrate on the medium; the other part—"the Christian"—would have him neglect his medium so long as he delivers the message. Neither works. The first produces nullity, the second produces propaganda. Both nullity and propaganda may have their appeal, but they are not art.

Amateur dramatics have come in for a lot of scorn and criticism from professionals who should know better. At their worst they are simply bad, and so is professional theater. At their best they can rival the professionals. Love covers a multitude of sins, and a competent amateur who loves the theater is better than a competent professional who sees it as a mere job. The difference *can* be one of talent and expertise, but it is just as likely to be one of full-time or part-time. But the point is that they do it because they love it—they understand it; they know it. How many Christians can say the same? Is it not too often a bandwagon or a duty? As Coleridge said, nothing great was ever achieved without enthusiasm. We should first of all love, and then we will not be in so much danger of selling our birthright for a pot of message.

Murray Watts—wishing as much as I do that it were otherwise—has said:

> Many a Christian has drifted from fellowship, discouraged by the misunderstanding and misinterpretation of his efforts. His freedom is often called in question. He becomes more acceptable the nearer he approaches evangelistic communication, in fact, the more recognizably functional his art becomes. When it has no clearly identifiable function, as in the case of an abstract painting, it mystifies; when a play is open-ended, refusing to pass judgment or offer a clear moral, it becomes sub-Christian in the eyes of the zealous. Such people would seize the arts and use them like blunt instruments to club the secular mind into submission. In actual fact, the sincere agnostic is repelled by such transparent manipulation.[2]

This attitude, too, accounts for the loss of the dramatic equivalent to the alabaster pot of ointment that was poured over

Christ's feet. The gratuitous, beautiful gesture. The response, "How beautiful!" is replaced by the response, "How many scalps?" The "thing of beauty" instead of being "a joy forever" is reduced to a tool for an hour.

We seem to have left our imaginary Questioner far behind, along with his burning question about where ideas come from, but maybe we have discovered something on the way: that "ideas" are not the simple equivalent of "messages," and that they are more likely to come in response to a loving call than a dutiful one.

There is, of course, a difference between where ideas come from and how ideas come. Let us take them separately and see if there is anything to be said on the subject.

A dictionary definition of the word "idea" is not necessary to us, but it is worth asking whether we mean by the word something more like a message or something more like a method. One can have an idea for a format without knowing what it is going to say, or one can have an idea of what subject we are going to tackle without much idea of how to go about it. If the two can arrive in the writer's brain as one seamless garment, so much the better—and it does happen, though not very often.

Again and again we come back to the inescapable truth: the more one knows, the more one has read, the greater is one's scope of choice. Many of my own ideas have come—sometimes after a long period of lying dormant in some cobwebby attic of the imagination, but filed away carefully by the subconscious—from an argument in an essay I have read, an episode in a novel, or an image in a poem. An idea can come from a chance remark in a discussion or from something glimpsed from a railway carriage. What they won't do is label themselves on arrival as *an idea*. They don't arrive like the cake in *Alice in Wonderland* with "Eat me" or "Use me" engraved upon them. They arrive simply as vivid but inchoate fragments of experience. It may even be that a proper definition of a writer has little to do with his technique but a lot to do with his capability for perceiving, remembering, and, subsequently, synthesizing what seem to be unconnected images and episodes into a coherent structure.

Ideas can even come from mistakes. A verbal slip during rehearsal can open a door into a completely new set of ideas and inferences. Even an ink-blot can have a lot to teach us. This is the composer Rossini writing to Louis Engel:

> When I was writing the chorus in G minor, I suddenly dipped my pen into the medicine bottle instead of the ink; I made a blot, and when I dried it with sand it took the form of a natural, which instantly gave me the idea of the effect which the change from G minor to G major would make, and to this blot all the effect—if any—is due.

The one place where ideas are least likely to be born is in the story told you by a stranger who prefaces his tale with a remark such as, "You're a writer—you could make a marvelous sketch out of this . . ."

What has to be done, as with the hatching of eggs, or the multiplication of bacteria, is to provide an atmosphere in which ideas are able to breed and grow. How this is done will alter from writer to writer. Some like to put themselves into an almost hermetically sealed room with a pen and paper. Some lie in the sun and doze. Some listen to music; some need total silence. Some eat and relax; some fast and are alert. Some walk up and down and scratch; some sit and scowl.

My wife, Hilary, has suggested that I dedicate my first book to the coffee producers of Columbia, and there is a lot of sense in that, but I also find a long bath conducive to ideas—candlelight, too, and staring at the large and beautiful horse-chestnut at the end of our garden. Sometimes I simply go and read some poetry or watch bowling on television. I dare say some people might find dipping their feet in lukewarm tea and rubbing their foreheads with egg-plant a help. One just cannot legislate in these matters. To an outsider the means seem to have no connection with the end, but to the writer they are of great importance. Each must find his own way.

Even without ideas, the craft of the writer must be practiced continually. Inspiration may come, but if, when it does, you have no vessel in which to hold it, it will slip away. One way of doing this might be to borrow books from the library—it doesn't matter whether they are novels, plays, poems, or non-fiction—find some-body to read to you the first couple of lines of a chapter, or perhaps the first exchange of words in a play, and then continue it yourself for a page or so. Those first two lines will imply an idea or a situation which should be enough to give you a bit of creative impetus. You don't need your own ideas, but you will soon find out whether you have any imagination. The very act of doing this may give you further ideas for a situation or a theme which you can use in your own work.

The reading of literature, which I have so strongly urged in this chapter, is best done as an end in itself. It was written to be read for pleasure and some sort of edification, and that is how it will work best. But to subject it to a detailed criticism is the way to find out how it works, why it works, how the writer gets his effects, why he moves us in just the way he does.

I suppose I had better be careful here in my use of the word criticism, for many regard it as a polite way of saying "raising objections." That is not at all what is meant by the word when used in a literary sense. Literary criticism is simply the analysis of a text—something which, under the title "comprehension," we are all taught to do at school, an equivalent to the surgeon's class in anatomy. Of course, the surgeon may come across a diseased pancreas or a hardened artery which will arouse a disapproving tut-tut. We may, in our literary surgery, come across a flabby construction or an inept image which will make us critical in the other sense, but the purpose of our dissection is knowledge, not approval or disapproval.

The best form of literary criticism is also the best fun; it is parody (by which I mean the conscious imitation of somebody else's style). There is another form which also goes under the name of parody, where certain words of the original passage are replaced by others, in order to poke fun, as in Lewis Carroll's version of "Twinkle, twinkle, little star":

> Twinkle, twinkle, little bat!
> How I wonder what you're at!
> Up above the world you fly,
> Like a teatray in the sky.

But this is not really parody at all. It is properly called burlesque. It is extremely tedious unless it is exceptionally well done, in which case it is only fairly tedious. Parody, however, is an art because, to do it well, the writer has had to understand how the mind of the original writer works, and that requires a great deal of knowledge and a large amount of sympathy—if not love. Parodies done in spite are often too extreme—more of a scream than a statement. But to write a good parody makes you ask all the right questions: what image would he have chosen for that? what would he have thought of that? are those words in his vocabulary? and so on. A good parody should be easily mistakable for the real thing. It is instructive and enjoyable to try writing a famous scene in a play in the style of three or four different playwrights.

As an inveterate parody writer myself, I was interested to read W. H. Auden's specimen curriculum in his daydream College for Bards:

1. In addition to English, at least one ancient language, probably Greek or Hebrew, and two modern languages would be required.

2. Thousands of lines of poetry in these languages would be learned by heart.

3. The library would contain no books of literary criticism, and the only critical exercise required of students would be the writing of parodies.

4. Courses in prosody, rhetoric, and comparative philology would be required of all students, and every student would have to select three courses out of courses in mathematics, natural history, geology, meteorology, archaeology, mythology, liturgics, cooking.

5. Every student would be required to look after a domestic animal and cultivate a garden plot.[3]

It is not that much different from the life of a medieval monk. It would certainly sort out the dilettantes from those who really felt they were being driven toward literature as a means of effective expression.

I have used the word "expression" there for the first time in connection with writing. The avoidance of the word has been deliberate, for it is a dangerous one to use. "Art is self-expression" people say, and think they have said it all, whereas they have not really said anything worth listening to. The "Art is self-expression" line is just another manifestation of that spirit that prizes originality above authenticity and modernity above all. The artist—so runs the argument—must be true to his subjective sensations and feelings; so what *he* does must be admired, not because it is intrinsically admirable, but because it is an expression of *his* personality, *his* uniqueness. That is a recipe for quirky, cranky, egotistic emptiness if there ever was one.

Yes, of course art has something to do with self-expression, but anybody who has had a child can tell you that self-expression is not necessarily art. The word that seems to fit the process of artistic creation—certainly far more appropriately than "expression"—is "exploration."

Exploration implies that one does not start with a pre-ordained message and try to embody it in a form, nor that one starts with a form ("I want to write a sonnet") and finds a subject to fit it, but that idea, form, and content grow together, the one influencing the other while the writer acts as a sort of marshall or ringmaster.

A painter, for instance, sits down to paint some trees not in order to give his future audience an aesthetic experience which he can get simply by looking at the trees themselves, but because the experience only starts to be realized during the actual process of painting. It is an exploration of the subject and of the artist's response to it.

This is just as true of writing: one writes about a subject in order to see it. This doesn't happen properly, of course, for the writer who refuses to be authentic—he confuses himself with his attitudes or his desire to write in such and such a way. Finally, his own scribbles come between him and the subject, and he can only see the mess he is making. In the worst cases, some uncritical observer then, in order to be encouraging, tells him how good it is and the writer is forever confirmed in his haphazard insincerities.

The mind tends to fall into one of two classes: the imaginative or the dogmatic. That is, it either explores or it asserts. It would probably be wrong to go quite as far as to say that the difference between the two is the difference between thinking and not thinking, but it is not too far from the truth.

Put an object into someone's hands and ask what they think of it, and you will get one of two responses: either a stock response

("I don't like those," "I'm not interested in that sort of thing," "Oh, my brother gave me one—they're awful!") which, in my classification is the dogmatic; or an imaginative response, which is difficult to exemplify here but which shows that they are able to look at it objectively, to explore it and let their imaginations loose on it.

What is interesting is that God has never required this stock response from us. St. Paul puts it this way: "For the invisible things of him from the creation of the world are clearly seen, being understood by the things that are made, even his eternal power and Godhead." That is an imaginative response demanded by creation, not a stock one. Paul Burbridge put it strikingly when he said that God does not put texts on the rose petals or on the sides of the mountains. Evangelical Christians tend not to go along with God on this one; they print beautiful posters of lakes and waterfalls, and then they pin us to a stock response by adding a Bible verse. The verse or the picture by itself might well open a door but the two together close all doors, make us see the one only as an illustration of the other and lock us to a stock response.

Nor did the incarnation demand a stock response. After hearing a parable the common man was not thereby bound to a definable attitude. Very often the only explanation he got was, "He who has ears to hear, let him hear." Christ was not recognizably the Son of God except to those who had the eyes to see.

In a similar way, theater does not browbeat a man into accepting a rule or message written in flaming letters on stone. Rather it opens his eyes and enlarges his sympathies. If it is written in anything, it is written in water; it soaks in and nourishes the parts that otherwise would not be reached.

What we have arrived at is a state of mind very close to that which Keats defined as Negative Capability. It was for this quality that he gave Shakespeare particular praise and, indeed, is as good an identification of where the Shakespearian genius actually lies as any. He defines Negative Capability like this: "When a man is capable of being in uncertainties, mysteries, doubts, without any irritable reaching after fact and reason."[4] In other words, not to impress himself upon things but to allow them to impress themselves upon him.

It is the imagination that shows us the truth of what is going on around us. It is imagination that makes art not a copy of life, not a snapshot, but an appraisal, a vision, sometimes a prophecy.

Notes

1. C.S. Lewis, *The Discarded Image*. Cambridge University Press, 1964.

2. I.M. Watts, *Christianity and the Theatre*. Edinburg: Handsel Press, 1986.

3. W.H. Auden, "The Poet and the City" from *The Dyer's Hand*. New York: Random House, 1962.

4. M. Buxton Foreman, *The Letters of John Keats* (2 volumes). Oxford University Press, 1931.

7

<u>More Writing</u>

Most people won't realize that writing is a craft.
You have to take your apprenticeship in it like
anything else.

Katherine Anne Porter, *Saturday Review*

*P*erhaps a better epigraph to this chapter would have been the words of Hilaire Belloc: "Of all fatiguing, futile, empty trades, the worst, I suppose, is writing about writing." I can understand his weariness, but it *can* be done profitably; hints can be given, pitfalls pointed out, and some lessons learned from experience passed on. That is what I shall try to do in this chapter. At the same time I make no apology for the length of the previous one. One must think before acting—offstage as well as on.... And it is far better to make one's own analysis of the past masters and to follow one's own tastes than to be spoon-fed by a stranger.

It is also worth pointing out that theater does not reside only in the short sketch. I realize that many people will be reading this book for the very purpose of creating short sketches, and I know that there are good reasons, on the whole, for choosing that form. What I am going to say about writing for the stage will be as applicable to the invention of sketches as to anything else, but the sketch has limitations:

1. It is not, by any means, despite its apparent simplicity, the easiest of forms to master.

2. It is necessarily limited to material of a humorous or at least a light nature.

3. It is not as effective as a full-length play which uses at least some of the resources of "theater" as opposed to "drama."

4. It has been done many, many times before.

Now, none of those arguments is a conclusive reason for bringing down the shutters on the performance of sketches. For a start, counter-arguments could be produced; probably many of them would have to do with time, concentration span, acceptability, and resources. But, at the same time, it is worth taking as objective and unprejudiced a look as is possible at what we are trying to explore, for whose sake, and how effective it really is.

It may just be that one full-length play, worked through properly and devised with skill and commitment, would be a better investment of time and resources than three short sketches over three months performed in a church with bad sightlines and impossible acoustics.

The sketch is to theater as a limerick is to poetry: a miniature form, crisp, short, and pointed. But good sketches, like good limericks, are notoriously hard to write. The best ones are little ounces of wisdom extracted from tons of experience. The worst are simply banal or trite—little ounces of pre-packed morality extracted from tons of well-meaning.

The sketch form needs to be a distillation and a contraction to essentials. It needs to be neat. It needs to be unforeseeable. It needs to be totally convincing even when it approaches the symbolic. It needs to have a distinctive flavor. It needs to be precise. It needs no padding or extraneous matter. It needs to leave the audience feeling that that was the ideal, even the unique, means of presentation. Now, all those qualities are not easily going to be achieved by the beginner. They are the fruit of long apprenticeship. Yes, of course the same *could* be said of a full-length play, but a failure of any one or two of those qualities in a long work will be much more acceptable and much less likely to throw the whole thing off-balance.

Actually, a long play does not have to be nearly so vigorous as that. Anyone who has seen *Amadeus*, for instance, will have realized that there are parts where the concentration is allowed, even encouraged, to flag or at least to change its quality. A scene which reaches profundity is followed by a light, silly scene, or by some music which demands a different sort of attention. There is delight in seeing something turn out as predicted; there is time for development and exploration of character; court room and music room, past and present are counterpointed; and anybody who knows about Mozart will know from the beginning how it is going to turn out. But a sketch cannot offer any alternatives to its single-minded drive from situation to resolution.

My second point about sketches, that they are limited to comedy rather than to the darker side of experience, may need a little explanation. I am not saying that comedy cannot be serious. In fact, I believe that there are some levels of seriousness that only those capable of comedy can reach. One of the most serious sketches I have written, on the far from laughable subject of adultery, is *A Man After My Own*.[1] But it is essentially a comic sketch. The laughter it provokes may be acid, but without the laughter it would be too solemn, too uncomfortable. Indeed, too banal; for the laughter at the end is what turns the whole sketch around, is what places the responsibility firmly, and is what shows up human nature for what it is.

What a sketch won't take is heavy drama. To start a sketch with a distraught woman rushing on stage screaming, "My baby! My baby! Oh, God, my baby!" is to be heading for a fall. Why? Because genuine tragedy stems from genuine character. So does the best comedy, of course, but comedy can work with stereotypes, with caricature. Tragedy can't. And the very form of the sketch precludes the creation of real, understandable, believable characters. Everything happens too quickly, and so any emotions portrayed become false emotions and, therefore, laughable. If you don't give your audience room for laughter in your sketches, they will find it for themselves and you will be left with an embarrassing anticlimax.

In some respects, one of the most damaging criticisms that the church can make of much modern theater is that it is superficial. It can command the finest skills, craft, talent, and resources, but, all too often, it has nothing to say. And again, all too often, the church has plenty it can say but has not found the skills or the sensitivity to say it. The real trouble begins when the church, by producing a four-minute sketch on the beatitudes with two male students in black leotards and the lady who does the flowers because she can't say "no," thinks that it has joined the battle. It has not even found the call-up papers.

We have already discussed how inspiration and ideas can arrive from almost anywhere: from a seed embedded, unconsciously perhaps, by a news item, a character or an episode in a book. But the working out of that idea as a piece of theater has to be done by means of techniques that are purely theatrical. That is where the real work starts, and it is probably particularly hard work because nobody ever seems to study how to write dramatically while they are at school. We read plays, and we dissect them and talk about their themes and so forth, but we are not encouraged to try it for ourselves as we are encouraged to write essays or stories. It is a great pity, for to try to write a play will immediately teach us just how skillful a business it really is. Just as reading will help us to write, so writing will help us to read with a more appreciative and understanding eye.

If we are honest, are not the best things we ever wrote, the purple passages we look back on with so much pride—tinged, of course, with a touching humility—are they not all descriptive? Or persuasive? A description of an old house, or a bank holiday at the seaside, or a train journey, or a favorite hobby. Well, there is nothing wrong with that, but if we think that is the way in which words are used we are in for quite a shock when we come to write for the theater. All our descriptive skills will suddenly go for nothing, unless a character is to recall, say, a scene from his childhood, or to look out of a window and describe what he sees. But even then we must be careful to do that only because it is required and not just because we think we are rather good at it.

Words on the stage behave in a very different way from words on the page of a book. Perfectly safe, well-brought-up words suddenly look stilted; words which the English teacher would have underlined as vulgar or colloquial are suddenly just what is needed. It is, to use one of those very expressions, a whole new ballgame. Like juggling. Which is also very difficult.

The theater does not rely on words. Words are only one facet of the theatrical experience. Theater is words, silence, action, symbol; a constantly shifting sequence of impressions. A sudden gesture, a long silence, or the slow fading of the lights may say much more than words.

A girl puts on her hat, carefully. Before she leaves, a young man makes a long speech at the end of which she takes off her hat and sits down again. Is not this a neater, more telling way of having her say, "I find you much more interesting than I thought" than if she were actually to use those words?

The dialogue is a kind of scaffolding within which and around which the actors and directors build the play. The clever writer is the one who does not put everything he wants to say into words. He sees the acting going on as he writes and puts his meaning into many different vessels.

Sometimes, for instance, the fact that a question is not answered gives the answer very plainly. Here is a bit of hack dialogue, but it will suffice to show what I mean:

> *He:*   I suppose what you're trying to say is that you
>   don't love me any more. (*Silence*) Would you
>   like another drink?
> *She:*   Yes, I'll have another drink.

The silence instead of a reply is, technically, ambiguous; she doesn't actually say whether or not she loves him. We, the audience, are thrown back on times when we have kept silence; we understand her reticence—such questions are unanswerable. It *is* a "no" . . . and yet . . .

Suddenly the audience is participating, not just being told things or even shown things. The audience understands. They've been through it. After such a silence, her "Yes. I'll have another drink" takes on the quality of a sigh, as if to say, "Is that all you can think about?"

Now substitute for that silence the stage-direction "She smiles," and see what a different scene you have created.

The words used in dialogue have to be chosen very carefully. Hidden feelings, reservations, half-truths have to be indicated concretely: the playwright has not got the novelist's luxury of being able to interpret or explain for half a page or so. In a novel you can say "she lied" or "he said, without really meaning it." How can you do that on the stage? Only through dialogue and inflection of the voice, through movement or stillness. The playwright must see what is going on upon the stage. This, incidentally, explains why reading a play without a fair amount of theatrical understanding or experience can be so deadly boring; half the significance is lost. Coming from a theatrical family, I had the advantage, even at the age of eleven, of having watched several Shakespeare plays in rehearsal and subsequent performance, and of being in a couple, before meeting Shakespeare on the printed page at school. I knew how it worked; I knew where the drama was to be found; I could not understand how anyone had problems with Shakespeare. I understand now. Had we all been taken to see a play before being asked to read it, we would have enjoyed it much more.

The exploratory process rather than the expository process, that is, working through rather than merely saying, is a prime necessity in dialogue. People do not talk in literary English; most people do not talk in measured phrases, or even coherently. There is no need for the dramatist to be incoherent, but he must write words that could have been used by those particular people in that situation.

Imagine two workmen having a coffee-break.

One:	Why did you laugh?
Two:	Because I thought of something very funny.

That is dialogue written by a writer who wants to get to the funny part. The information is fine and the words are quite possible to speak, but it has not prepared the audience to laugh; it has not led them, enjoyably, to a point where they are ready for a joke. Another version:

One:	(Laughs quietly)
Two:	What's up?
One:	Huh?
Two:	What you chuckling about?
One:	Me?
Two:	Yeah.
One:	No, I was just thinking . . .

That does the same job with more theatrical tact. It allows the characters to establish themselves just a tiny bit. It sets up the situation; it intrigues a little. It is two people, not two mouthpieces.

If a playwright is continually writing lines that could be spoken by anybody on the stage, there is something wrong with his writing. He is conveying information and not letting his characters live and do their work. Character is more important than message. Message is the seed that must be dropped on the ground and allowed to die; character is the means by which the message will be given back to you, alive and significant.

Once a couple of characters are established in the author's mind, dialogue should be able to flow more freely. He can explore the conversations as they take place—how would A react to that remark? Does that put B on the spot? Does C know about this? Didn't A tell him something entirely different?

It is worth letting go at times like this and seeing what happens. Editing can always be done later.

It is a good rule never to write a line that you could not say yourself. Actors have a hard enough job as it is without writers giving them impossible or embarrassing dialogue to speak. It is a fairly good guide, though not a perfect one, that if the actors find the dialogue difficult to remember, there is probably something wrong with it. It may be slightly unnatural; maybe there is a step in the argument which has been left out; maybe one or two sentences are in the wrong place.

A good line will follow logically from the one before it; a very good line will also follow logically, but may not appear to. An excellent line may be something which cuts through the whole scene and changes the pace.

A good line will tell you one—or more—of five things:

1. Something about the character who speaks.
     His way of putting things
     His particular sort of understatement
     His particular overworked phrase
     His annoying attitude, etc.

2. Something about the character spoken to.
     He is not respected

He is generally feared
He is not to be trusted with the whole truth, etc.

3. Something about the character or situation spoken about. (But this may not be true owing to the above.)

4. It furthers the plot, intrigue, action of the play.

5. It can be ironic if, for instance, the audience knows more than the character does.

The same thing, of course, goes for silence or movement. It must always be appropriate to the character or it will be seen for what it is—a device.

Perhaps it is worth asking at this point what may seem to be a very obvious question, but one that few people seem to have answered for themselves. What is dramatic? What does the word mean? What sort of events on stage are we justified in calling "dramatic" events? Let us forget for the moment the use that tabloid press gives to the word and think purely in theatrical terms. Unfortunately, it is almost impossible to do that. As soon as the word "drama" or "dramatic" hits the grey cells, other words immediately attach themselves unbidden: a dramatic escape—teacher in cliff drama—dramatic change of fortune for heiress—motorcycle ban drama rocks town council. But if these incidents were to be relived for us on stage, probably the only one to be dramatic in a theatrical sense would be the first. The second may have been dramatic but was more likely to have been simply dangerous. The third incident probably means little more than "quick" or "surprising," and it is unlikely that the last means anything more than a small squabble.

Theatrically what is dramatic is what stops the audience coughing, what makes them sit on the edge of their seats, what makes them follow or wait upon the action with a new degree of urgency. A killing on the stage is not necessarily dramatic. It may be exciting, unexpected, but the act itself is not intrinsically dramatic; nor, even, would be an airplane coming through the roof, for drama lies in instability, in the changing of impressions, not in a static action however loud, prolonged, or violent. When impressions are changing, then the audience, as it were, pursues them; the pursuit becomes urgently fascinating. Drama is, if you like, the possibility of surprise rather than the surprise itself; for once a question is answered it is dead, and another has to be posed. Theater has to propose, then elaborate and sustain a question all the time.

The word "conflict" is often used in the context of drama and what it is all about. Perhaps it is rather a strong word in some ways; it certainly fits the Shakespearian tragedy, it fits *Minder* and *Witness for the Prosecution*, but with Ayckbourn, Frayn, N. F. Simpson, and so on it is more difficult to apply. The word "intrigue" might be more appropriate. The audience needs to be in a state of pleasurable tension if the play is to work.

An example of the distinction between excitement and drama is to be found in my own play for children *Angel at Large*. Toward the end of the play, Maximus and Tychicus—two of Herod's soldiers detailed to kill all the children in Bethlehem—discover a baby, *the* baby, though they don't know it, at the inn. An extended and very complicated chase ensues, invoking the soldiers, the innkeeper's daughter with the baby, Joseph, an angel called Auriel, and a camel called Desmond. It gets faster and more furious; not a bottom in the audience is touching a seat. At the end of the chase the soldiers actually get the baby; Maximus holds him and the two soldiers begin cooing over him and giving him their fingers to squeeze and all the things people do with babies. So we've had excitement and we've had a bit of a surprise; but the drama comes when the innkeeper's daughter hands them a sword and tells them to get on with what they came for. It is a wonderful moment. After the hullabaloo and laughter, how do you get a complete and utter silence for as long as you like from seven-year-olds? Teachers might say it can't be done. But drama can do it. That sudden, new tension creates a perfect silence which will last even after Max has made this decision.

As a contrast, if you leave no unanswered questions, if there is no intrigue, you end up with flat, meaningless mush:

Nicodemus:	I never thought it could happen.
Joseph:	No.
Nicodemus:	But now it has happened.
Joseph:	Yes, now it has happened.
Nicodemus:	The Son of God crucified on Calvary.
Joseph:	Between two thieves.
Nicodemus:	It's impossible, and yet . . .
Joseph:	It has happened. What was it that he called out as he died?
Nicodemus:	"My God, my God, why has thou forsaken me!"
Joseph:	The words of David in Psalm 22.
Nicodemus:	It's almost as if he was taking upon himself all the sins of the world, and those sins had separated him from God.
Joseph:	Yes. I know what you mean.
Nicodemus:	And now it's all over. He is dead.
Joseph:	And we are alive.
Nicodemus:	All the things, all the amazing things he did and said have come to this!
Joseph:	What was it he said to you, Nicodemus, when you went to see him that time?
Nicodemus:	He said, "Verily, verily, I say unto thee, except a man be born of water and the spirit he cannot enter into the kingdom of God. That which is born of the flesh is the flesh, and that which is born of the spirit is spirit. Mar-

	vel not that I said unto thee, Thou must be born again. The wind bloweth where it listeth, and thou hearest the sound thereof, but canst not tell whence it cometh: so is every one that is born of the spirit."
Joseph:	Ah.
Nicodemus:	Well, it's the end of a long day.
Joseph:	Yes, it is.
Nicodemus:	I'm ready for bed.
Joseph:	So am I.
Nicodemus:	I don't think any of us will ever forget this day.
Joseph:	No. Nor do I. Nor do I.

The audience on the other hand, will do their best to forget the sketch as soon as they can. Hopefully nobody reading that could mistake it for a piece of theater: it is dull, trite, predictable, undramatic, pompous, and hideously flat. But let us analyze its badness in detail so that we are not tempted to make similar mistakes with just a little more subtlety.

1. The dialogue is unspeakable—literally and metaphorically. Nobody, except in Christian sketches, speaks so measuredly or unemotionally.

2. There is no character, no observation, no truth to life, no sense of real grief. This is bad American film-epic dialogue further emasculated by a timid and superficial spirituality. The "noble" repetitions of the first four lines are empty. The completion of the sentence in line 8 is totally misjudged: it would be a banal enough device to fade out as Nicodemus does, but it is a sure way of getting a laugh to repeat "it has happened" yet again.

3. The sketch adds nothing to this statement: Jesus died on the cross and his followers were distraught. It actually takes away from the statement because the followers are not seen to be distraught, merely dull-witted.

4. Notice the "Teaching Points" carefully inserted: the reference to Psalm 22, the doctrinal teaching of what happened on the cross, the unnatural introduction of Jesus' teaching on conversion.

5. And how unnaturally this is quoted, word-perfect from a photographic memory at such a time! What response could one make to that? The "Ah" is bound to get a laugh. Is there anything that would not?

6. The pseudo-dramatic repetition of the last line is the last straw, but the whole of the ending is only a limp device to get off the stage.

7. Where is the intrigue? Where is the conflict? Where is the climax? Where is the point?

It is not even worth rewriting this sketch as an exercise, for, as I have suggested in #3 above, the whole thing is misconceived. This tells us nothing about the ministry of Christ, nothing about the crucifixion except that it happened and nothing about the two speakers. The only point there can be in retelling a story in dramatic form is to shed light on character and motivation. Otherwise the story is best read in the original. I think it is true to say, however, that many pastors are as responsible for bad sketches as the writer or the actors are. If a pastor understands how theater works there is no problem, but there are some who might well have commissioned the above sketch, asking for the teaching points to be put in, demanding that anything biblical should be quoted verbatim, and being extremely uneasy about any fictional element.

But the essence of theater is that it is fiction; that is its strength and its safeguard. We are close, here, to a very important point about our beliefs and our art which I should like to explore, not in the certainty that I shall be able to make my feelings totally comprehensible or even come to any definite conclusions, but simply because it is such a crucial issue.

I believe—and this is this year's belief; I may discover next year that I am wrong—that the raison d'être of art is to explore man's experience and vision of the world.

By that I mean not just the tangible realities of society, behavior, sex, kingship, cardboard boxes, nature, occupation, coffee pots, poverty, and all the other things one would expect the world to include; but the soul also, instinct, virtue, imagination, death, morality—the ineffable. But I am not sure that art can deal with God. I am not convinced that theology can deal with God. But art *can* deal with our desire for God, our rejection of God, our difference from God. Art must be man-centered because it is imaginative and fictional. Even if we go back to that word "expression," what art expresses is ideas, not facts. Dogma sits very uncomfortably on the shoulders of art.

Art may help us to understand ourselves and the situation we are in, but it cannot help us to understand God. If it teaches at all—and I'm sure it does sometimes—it teaches us by showing and revealing, not by ordering or telling. Art never makes us an offer we can't refuse.

The "message," if you like, of the Christian artist has to be implied rather than stated if his artifact is to work in the way that art does work. In this way the members of the audience become creative participants too; they take what he has given them, and they draw their conclusions. They must be left free to agree or disagree with what the artist implies. All too often what an artist says is what we say he says. He might say something very different if we could ask him.

This is very easily discernible in the field of the visual arts. *Guernica* does not say that war is terrible—it shows us a picture. It is we who say that Picasso is saying, "War is terrible." What we mean is that that is the implication that we draw from it. It would have been so much less a work of art if Picasso had put on it a balloon coming from a mouth, and in that balloon the words, "War is terrible."

Our beliefs do not have to be stated in our work for that work to have a Christian significance. The effectiveness of our work in glorifying God comes from what we choose as material.

In the sketch about adultery, *A Man After My Own*, which I mentioned previously, none of the characters expresses any religious belief or any anti-religious belief. There is no pressure on the audience to accept any one particular version of the stories told as The Truth. And yet, adultery, simply by observing behavior and human nature, is revealed for what it is.

There is nothing wrong with preaching, but art does not preach, it shows. This is what H. Caudwell writes in *The Creative Impulse*:

There has been a constant and sometimes embittered argument about the precise place of the artist, and it is difficult adequately to define his function. His activity is in part that of teacher, philosopher, and entertainer. His position in society is vital but neglected. His contribution to the happiness of mankind has been greater and more lasting than that of any other class of man except, perhaps, the great religious teachers . . . His aim is unselfish: it is, fundamentally, to give delight to other men. All this he must realize and consider, guarding himself by logic against the dangers of becoming a charlatan, a preacher, a tradesman, or a buffoon.[3]

Humanity must always be the basis of art if art is to have any effect on us. To enact a sketch that says, "Jesus tells us to forgive" is not a lot of help to anybody unless they didn't know that to start with. A play that shows what forgiveness actually means in human terms demonstrates the truth that we want to teach.

To be truly spiritual, I believe, and to offer truly spiritual answers to the questions being posed today, we must get away from the sort of spirituality that thinks every situation is solved by a verse from the Bible. We must get away from the sort of simplistic drama that says the same thing. The Bible verse is the *beginning* of the solution, not the end. As people in the church we must forget pre-packaged doctrinal answers and learn to listen, to sympathize, and to identify with the suffering. Yes, in the light of those Bible verses, certainly. But what we must not do is hide in the shadows that they cast. And in our art let us step *from* the Bible into the world, however tremblingly; let us not be in continual retreat from the world back into the Bible.

What I am *not* saying is that writing with a direct message— what I have elsewhere distinguished from art by using the word "propaganda"—cannot be written and should not be written. I have written quite a bit of it myself. All I am saying is that, in the end, it is not so memorable or rich as art, and it does not go so far; it does not open doors in the imagination—it informs. The writer who limits himself to that sort of work, who restricts himself to assertions rather than explorations, will have fewer and fewer riches to draw on. He always runs the risk of being superficial, even of missing the point. The writer who produces propaganda as a kind of by-product of his art will be that much less likely to produce a sketch in the "Bad Samaritan" mold.[4]

The most important thing for us to do, as writers, is to tell the truth, for that is how God will best be glorified. We are not, as artists, concerned with parading our own Christianity—that is a subject for autobiography. What we should be concerned with is keeping our art authentic and leading others to the truth.

There has, from time to time, been discussion on whether Shakespeare was a Christian. Does it matter? Are the plays suddenly good if he was, and bad if he was not? Of course not. What a pity if we are attended to by some only if we advertise our beliefs, and by others if we hide them. The man who wrote:

Over the land freckled with snow half-thawed
The speculating rooks at their nests cawed
And saw from elm-tops, delicate as flower of grass,
What we below could not see, Winter pass.[5]

was a poet; that is all we need to know. It is as immoral for Christians to assert that art should be overtly expressive of belief as that the Soviet Union should demand that their art should express socialist realism. What a shameful thing it would be for the greatest philosophy in the world always to produce art more closely related to the television commercial than to the works of Shakespeare.

Theoretical and practical problems always go hand in hand, which is why I have felt it necessary to discuss the propaganda versus art question at such length. A new writer is usually advised, quite rightly, to start from his own experience and observation. Now this can prove quite difficult for a Christian writer as I know from my own experience. Many of the things which he is expected to write about are not within his experience: they are principles or concepts taken from the Bible. Well, of course that is perfectly reasonable and logical, but if those concepts are not really part of the writer's life and understanding, how is he to write about them adequately?

For such a young Christian, as I was when I was asked to write for church services and missions, it can be a real problem. Technique without knowledge can produce crass writing as easily as knowledge without technique. One is faced, suddenly, with these huge theological concepts such as "service," "temptation," "faith," "the peace of God"—and what is one to make of them? Here is Keats again: "Axioms in philosophy are not axioms until they are proved upon our pulses." You cannot reveal the truth unless you know the truth. Every church is looking for its C.S. Lewis, but Lewis was a man of many different sorts of experience allied to age and maturity. *The Screwtape Letters* were written out of a deep understanding of temptation which is, surely, beyond the scope of a nineteen-year-old English student. And yet it is very rare for a church drama group to contain anyone older than their late twenties. Drama is just for the young people. As long as congregations think in that way, the theater that their churches produce is bound to show a certain superficiality for which the writers are not entirely to blame.

These chapters cannot hope to be of very much practical help to writers except in so far as they direct thought and attention to the matters that need to be thought about and attended to. There are no rules that can be formulated that cannot be brilliantly broken by an outstanding writer. The practical hints, then, which I end with may prove useful as a starting point but must be ignored at the dictates of a greater good.

Dialogue

This is the skeleton of the play; if it is weak the body of the play will collapse. Dialogue reveals character; the words spoken by Colonel Oakes must be his words and his alone, just as Winifred Thripp is immediately recognizable by her idiom.

Listen to people talking on the bus, on the subway, in a shop. As a writer you will not be able to use such conversations verbatim; you will have to reduce and exaggerate. What elements will you keep? Remember that significant speech is not just words. Some people might clear their throats gently before they say something difficult, some might "hmmm" in response to anything anyone else contributes as a kind of shorthand for "I'm thinking about that." It can be a very overworked trick, but individuals all have their own idioms which can be used for good comic effect. There is a type of person who will always be coming out with, "Well, my mother always used to say . . ." or, "Let's examine that . . ." or, "I may be barking up the wrong tree, of course, but . . ." Do not be tempted to stick these on to normal dialogue in order to create character: they grow out of the right characters.

Have a look at how cleverly Michael Frayn uses dialogue. Small exaggerations, compressions, and repetitions have lifted this out of the realm of the merely tedious into the comic, even satiric. We do not even need to be told the situation: the dialogue tells all.

Buckle:	Poor old Jimmy.
Headingley:	Jimmy?
Buckle:	Jimmy McBride.
Headingley:	No!
Buckle:	Heart.
Headingley:	I didn't know that.
Buckle:	Yes.
Headingley:	Heart?
Buckle:	And drink.
Headingley:	Then there's poor old Arthur.
Buckle:	Yes, there's poor old Arthur.
Headingley:	Shock of my life.
Buckle:	Never have imagined.
Headingley:	Never dreamt.
Buckle:	What was it, in the end?
Headingley:	Five years.
Buckle:	Five years.
Headinglcy:	I don't really feel that I've changed.
Buckle:	No, I don't feel I have.
Headingley:	And yet in some ways . . .
Buckle:	Oh, in some ways . . .

Headingley:	In fact, it's surprising how *much* one has changed in some ways.
Buckle:	Oh, I'm astonished how much I've changed. In some ways. But also, how *little*.
Headingley:	But how funny being back here!
Buckle:	*Isn't* it funny?

* * *

Buckle:	You think you remember everything. Then when you look you realize there are all sorts of things you'd forgotten.
Headingley:	Funny thing, memory, isn't it?
Buckle:	Then, as soon as you see the things you'd forgotten, you realize you remember them after all.
Headingley:	Funny.
Buckle:	Very funny.
Headingley:	And then again in another way it's not funny at all.
Buckle:	No, it's all perfectly natural.
Headingley:	I think that's really what's so funny about it.[6]

The artificiality of the construction works beautifully because the bricks it is built with are so natural. A lesser writer would have been content with:

Headingly:	It was the shock of my life.
Buckle:	I'd never have imagined it.
Headingly:	No, I'd never have dreamt it.

But how much more character—and also satire—there is in Frayn's version.

In the same way that the writer has to keep his ears open for the idiom of the private person, he must also be able to reproduce that of the public figure. Occupations have their own phraseology, their own rhythms and unwritten syntaxes. Newsreaders, interviewers, weathermen, politicians, commentators, presenters all have their little ways. In a sketch, the reproduction of them must be absolutely sure: approximations will not do.

Remember, too, that people seldom talk in bursts of more than three or four sentences unless they are telling a story, reminiscing, or explaining something difficult. Even then it can sound awkward on the stage, especially if you need your audience to understand the explanation as well. Dialogue is also much easier to learn than monologue. Compare these two versions of what is, fundamentally, the same "information."

Version #1

> *Anselm:*   It's probably my fault if poor Brother Eyore is a little bit too sound in the statutes and not fainting quite enough for salvation. A man's nature can be changed if we create the sort of environment that shows him something better. After all, one sheep is more important than the ninety-nine. Sometimes I long for a Lindisfarne: seclusion, retreat, being apart—good-bye and good riddance to the twentieth century. It's different for you, of course, Antony: you were a priest. You're used to supermarkets, juggernauts, battered wives, all that sort of thing. I'm afraid of all that.

Version #2

> *Anselm:*   Poor Brother Eyore: a little bit too sound in the statutes and not fainting enough for salvation. It's probably my fault.

Antony:	Nonsense. Eyores are Eyores: you can't change a man's nature.
Anselm:	A man's nature can be changed.
Antony:	Only if he wants it to be.
Anselm:	And he'll only want it to be if we create the sort of environment that shows him something better.
Antony:	We've been over all this before, Father.
Anselm:	And you still won't agree that the one sheep is more important than the ninety-nine?
Antony:	*As* important, not more important.
Anselm:	Hmmmm. Sometimes I long for Lindisfarne. Don't you?
Antony:	I've never been there.
Anselm:	Oh, I don't mean Lindisfarne particularly. But seclusion, retreat, being apart.
Antony:	Good-bye twentieth century.
Anselm:	In the best way, yes. Good-bye and good riddance.
Antony:	Oh, no.
Anselm:	Ah, well! It's different for you, Antony. You were a priest.
Antony:	What difference does that make?
Anselm:	You're used to supermarkets, juggernauts, battered wives, all that sort of thing.
Antony:	How do they impinge on you?
Anselm:	They exist. Well, no, they don't impinge, as you put it. Not really. But the twentieth century is there. It yawns outside; you can't get rid of it.

The second version is not, in essence, superior to the first. It is slightly more developed; the ideas are "arrived at" rather than stated. If you wanted to be disapproving of it, you could say not that it was "developed" but that it was "diluted." That is true; but, remember, we are dealing with an aural medium here. The audience will hear the words, not see them; they need time, perhaps, to sink in. It is often forgotten that a play exists in time and space in a way that a novel does not. One can look back over a novel, remind oneself of an earlier incident, skip over or read more carefully. Not so in the theater: the pace of a play must not be faster than the audience's comprehension. Nor must it be slower, or it becomes tedious.

What the second version does is to give much more information about the relationship between Anselm and Antony: you can tell which is the older of the two, you can tell how much they respect each other despite their differences, you can tell whether Anselm is likely to be a despot or not, you can occasionally see the difference between wisdom and experience. And yet there is no judgment on the part of the writer: the audience is not told which of the two they should be identifying with—there are no good guys and bad guys, they are left simply to listen and become involved.

Good Guys and Bad Guys

The Bible often speaks in massive generalizations. The righteous man is compared with the unrighteous, the sinful with the sinless, the faithful with the faithless, the sheep with the goats. Yes, and only God has the right to differentiate and to speak in such terms; only God can see into the secrets of the human heart. We are told that it is not right to make such judgments on individuals. We can identify sin—if we have discernment—and condemn that, but people are different. We may criticize, but we may not blame.

This is a big problem for the Christian writer, especially for the writer of short sketches for performance in churches or as part of Christian teaching. To God, and in biblical terms, there is such a thing as a good or an evil person, a just or an unjust person. To us there cannot be. We are *all* sinful; as St. Paul says, we have fallen short of the glory of God. But as the truism says—and it would not be a truism if it were not true—there is good and bad in everyone. Sometimes we are faithful and sometimes we are not. Sometimes we are self-sacrificing, sometimes we are selfish and egocentric; we are both just and unjust; we lie, cheat, and hurt; we are honest, we are full of integrity, and we console.

So when we translate God's Word into drama, that is, when we apply it to people and situations and make it flesh, the Word becomes not just simple but simplistic. Truth, by the act of dramatization, becomes falsehood. We cannot portray on stage A Good Man. We can have a symbol for a good man, but we cannot have the thing itself. None of us knows, except in theory, what a good man is.

This is the real dilemma of the Christian artist. Because he is a Christian as well as an artist, he is asked to make statements which his art is incapable of making. Theater shows humanity in action. It is theology that shows God in action. A marriage of the two is bound, by its very nature, to be unjust to one or the other. Either it will be biblically true but artistically spineless and trite, or it will be artistically very powerful but very difficult to make sense of in a straightforward spiritual way.

It is not *true* that if a thing can be said it can be said just as well in theater, or dance, or in music, or in oils on canvas. A preacher often wants facts to be transmitted, but the arts are not vehicles for the transmission of facts. It is as if one were to say to a painter "paint me a picture of somebody doing nothing." It can't be done. You can imagine, in theory, somebody doing nothing; you can understand the concept of somebody doing nothing; but it is impossible to *show* somebody doing nothing.

So, the first thing to do when called upon to dramatize something abstract or very general is to make it as concrete as possible. Create a character who, by what he does or says, or by what he does not do or say, will raise the concept in people's minds. Forget about the concept itself. Character is the answer. In fact character itself, if we can look at it in this way, could be defined as a measure of falling

short of an ideal. A writer does not create an impatient man; it is
the audience who defines him as impatient; what the writer does
is to create a man with just so much patience. A writer does not
create a character with no self-control; he creates a character with
self-control that goes only so far. He creates; the audience judges.
It is this fundamentally sympathetic approach that allows the
writer to deal with black-and-white issues and yet never to have to
make such distinctions.

Let me illustrate what I mean from two of my own sketches. In
Christian terms, not to have believed in the Son of God—what he
did, what he said—is pretty well the ultimate wickedness: salvation cannot come if you do not at least believe. Therefore, in the
black-and-white terms of which we have been speaking, he who
does not believe is definitely a Bad Guy.

Now look at Hymie, the wine-waiter in *100% Proof.*[7] He falls
straight into that category. A miracle happens under his not incon-
siderable nose, and yet he refuses to be convinced. The sketch
works, I believe, because Hymie is *not* portrayed as a Bad Guy. He
is just like you and me—good-hearted, kind, friendly, reasonable,
ordinary. The sketch may say something about miracles, but it says
a lot more about human nature—about easy habits having to be
discarded before the truth can seep through, about miracles themselves not being of much use if the heart of man remains un-
changed, about the truth of Luke 16:31: "If they hear not Moses and
the prophets, neither will they be persuaded, though one rose from
the dead." If I had taken the Christian *attitude* and painted Hymie
as a Bad Guy, the sketch would not have worked. Starting, however, from the idea that Hymie is neither particularly good nor
particularly bad, one can arrive at a more truthful and objective
consideration of *his* attitude. The writer does not beg questions, he
shows. We discussed in the last chapter the idea of a question
answered being a question dead. That is as true of a character as it
is of a plot—indeed, it seems to me that that can be the only
meaning of the expression "character is plot." How Hymie will

react is the only interesting question in the sketch; if we are told he is a Bad Guy then that interest is taken away and the sketch is dead.

In another sketch, *Sharing the Joke* (see Appendix), I challenged myself to write a funny sketch about a man who had no sense of humor. The problem here is, how can you make an audience laugh at something which, by definition, is not funny? Again the answer is through character. A man who believes in himself when there is nothing to believe in is funny. The laughter comes through awareness of the gap between what the man thinks to be true and what actually is true. The fact that the gap happens to occur in the area of humor does not, then, matter. But the audience cannot have the lack of humor directed straight at them, or they'd get bored. If they are to react to the failing with objectivity, it must be directed at someone else. Therefore, although the sketch is a monologue, there are two people on the stage; the second man does not even look up from the book he is reading. He gives the audience, if you like, the sense of the ideal; he represents the lack of interest and lack of reaction which the other man inspires. Art, once again, is better than reality: anyone can stand up and bore an audience, but if you show an audience someone else being bored, it can be an entertaining and revealing experience.

I stated, above, that theater shows humanity in action. I believe that to be true even though the statement, as it stands, is open to question. One might say, for instance, that it ignores symbolic theater such as *Everyman* and a good many other medieval theater pieces as well as some modern ones.

My answer to that would be that it really only becomes good theater when it transcends its own forms or its own limitations. A lot of people reverence such plays because of their antiquity; they are part of our heritage and our tradition. Now that is an excellent starting point, but such feelings must be mixed with honesty. Let us ascribe to ancient things all the worth we can, but let us be truthful as well and not pretend to feelings that we do not have.

It seems to me that what people value most about such plays are the moments when they are least typical, when they are least like themselves. It is the touches of real, human feelings, of genuine, poetic insight, of modernity and humor suddenly appearing in the mouth of an abstraction such as "Virtue" or "Rumor" amid all the marble rhetoric, which suddenly convinces us that there is a breath of humanity here after all.

I am not saying that is the only reason for liking them. Nothing has ever been made that somebody did not genuinely love for itself and there are certainly going to be people who do love such pieces for themselves. I am simply confessing that I—and I suspect there are many like me—find them, on the whole, tedious. I know if I were offered tickets for *Everyman* or a new Stoppard play which I would choose.

There are certainly ways of dealing with the abstract idea by these symbolic means, but one must be aware, even more than usual, of being dull or of merely moralizing.

I was once asked to write a sketch about "The Body of Christ." This can be identified as the "Ulp" factor in Christian theater. It is the "Ulp!" factor which leads, if one is not careful, to the Cringe factor. But more of that later. The "Ulp!" factor is the feeling exhibited by a writer on being asked to condense 138 books (with footnotes) and ten years of sometimes contradictory Christian teaching into a three-minute sketch. If such a request is not within your experience, a similar effect can be obtained by imagining a friend handing you the telephone and saying, "It's the Internal Revenue Service—for you," or Evel Knievel telling you that you have to motorcycle-jump over five cars in December in front of 17 million viewers.

Now, no pastor should ever ask someone to write about "The Body of Christ." It is not only unfair, it is silly. It is like an impresario asking a playwright for a play about "Life"—it is simply not a definite subject.

In the end I did write one, having pinned down the subject to something more like, "The Worth of the Individual," and I did it by using characters with something of the symbolic about them. I used angels.

This seems to contradict what I said just now about Good Guys and Bad Guys being identified and therefore diminishing the effect. But, if one treats those Good-Guys-Beyond-Question in a very human way, a kind of double vision can be obtained. You know they are telling the truth, because they are angels; they can represent the Ideal, and therefore the thoughts and opinions they have about men and women take on a very satirical, objective flavor. At the same time it can be fun listening to angels talking and displaying those human characteristics which are so attractive in the *Everyman* type of play. One can do just the same, in reverse, with devils. It would be false and silly to invent a kind of Perfect Man, but angels are ideally situated between Man and God to avoid the complications of human motives and ideas on the one hand, and the danger of a kind of blasphemy on the other.

Angels are immediately identifiable beings in a Christian context, but the same distancing can be used for satiric effect by using Greek or Norse gods or even famous departed souls. In *A Dig at the Twentieth Century* I have actually used human beings, but, since they are from the future, an extra degree of knowledge and moral improvement can be presupposed.

Translating the Bible

All writing means something. It is very hard to write anything that manages entirely to escape significance unless it is undertaken merely as an exercise. Even an exercise in the hands of a real writer will be more than the sum of its parts. In the Bible we have an example, par excellence, of a book which was intended to mean something and if our dramatizations of it are to have any significance we must know both what the Bible is saying and what it means. The two things are not always the same, either in literary criticism or in biblical analysis.

Subject matter and theme are separate entities and yet are inextricable one from another. Often the subject matter, the story, if you like, can be enjoyed without any conscious recognition of the theme. A good example of this is *The Lion, the Witch and the Wardrobe* by C.S. Lewis. The story is a modern fairy tale of four children who enter a magic world through the back of a wardrobe and end up in an amazing adventure with dwarves, witches, trolls, and talking animals. The theme is the redemption of the world.

But until church leaders are enlightened enough to allow actors to perform plays in church simply because they are good in themselves, we are going to have to address ourselves to the problems of finding the theme (or teaching-point as it is often called) of a story or a Bible passage and putting that into dramatic form.

A simple retelling of the story is usually not enough. There are many reasons for this. Sometimes it is that, in a narrative for instance, the significance will not come over in a simple re-enactment and the story needs to be framed within a context that brings out the meaning. Sometimes it is that the teaching, as in a Pauline Epistle for instance, is theoretical (*all* significance!) and needs to be diluted and fleshed out in a dramatic situation. My sketch *Jonah's Journey*, for children, is an example of the first, and so, really, is *100% Proof*; Paul Burbridge's sketch *Spreading the Word Around a Bit* is a good example of the second. The meaning of the original passage has to be clearly understood before it can be translated for the stage.

But there is another problem, and that is when a Bible story has become like a dead metaphor and needs to be revived. A dead metaphor is a figure of speech which is a metaphor but which has been used so often that it no longer carries the force of the original picture—it has become a form of words. Thus, we may talk about a ship plowing through the waves, but the visual image of a real plowshare cutting a furrow has gone; it is just something we always say when talking about ships. In the same way there are many passages in the Bible—often those which would have been most vivid when they were first used—that have become over-familiar to Christians and are even positively obscure to those who hear them for the first time. These are the ones that need putting into modern dress—often literally—and refreshing.

The most famous example of this is Murray Watts' *The Parable of the Good Punk Rocker*. It was originally written in order that the force of the parable of the Good Samaritan might be regained. The word "Samaritan" has, to a modern ear, no vestige of the disgust and hostility it would have aroused in a Jewish ear at the time of Christ. We have, in fact, come to think of Samaritans as good, kindly, self-sacrificing people. If that flavor is allowed to tinge the parable it becomes meaningless. When *The Parable of the Good Punk Rocker* was first performed it did precisely what was hoped: it renewed the force of the story by contrasting a modern outcast with the self-satisfied members of "decent society."

It is an interesting comment on Christian thought that although punk rock and that era has passed as quickly as such fashions do, and the Punk Rocker is himself almost as dead a metaphor as the Samaritan, the sketch is still being performed without revision.

To find ways of translating the Bible is actually a much easier task than to think of ideas. When Jesus, for instance, says, "The kingdom of heaven is like this . . ." we need to go just that step further and continue "and that is a bit like this . . ." It is a matter of understanding the passage and then looking for an equivalent to the image Jesus uses when that is necessary. It is quite a good exercise to look through the parables and see how they could be translated. Ideas breed ideas, so it is worth tackling all of them even if, like the pearl of great price or the talents or the sower and the seed, they are perfectly understandable in their present form.

Simplicity

The hallmark of a good sketch is that it says one thing, and it says it well. If too many subjects are tackled they obscure one another, and the pace and direction of the sketch is lost. A line you write may remind you of something else you could say on the subject, or a joke you could make, or an aside for the initiated. Try not to be tempted. There is no room for sub-plot in three minutes, or even in ten. There should be a logical, discernible development from beginning to end; any interruption must be germane to the argument or the style. If the sketch you are writing breeds so many other ideas, you are very fortunate; you can use them to write ten good sketches instead of putting them all together to make one bad one.

Let me end this chapter by reiterating my plea not to start with a moral or a teaching point unless you are really obliged to. Don't be tempted to ask yourself what your audience needs and then try to give it to them; you will almost certainly end up brandishing attitudes rather than creating drama. One of the greatest rewards of being an exploratory writer, rather than one who merely regurgitates principles that he has learned, is that you can learn from your own writing. The following passage is concerned with writings for children, but it makes just as good sense if for "children" you substitute the word "audiences":

I might be asked, "Do you equally reject the approach which begins with the question, 'What do modern children need?' In other words, with the moral or didactic approach?" I think the answer is Yes. Not because I don't like stories to have a moral: certainly not because I think children dislike a moral. Rather because I feel sure that the question, "What do modern children need?" will not lead you to a good moral . . . Let the pictures tell you their own moral. For the moral inherent in them will rise from whatever spiritual roots you have succeeded in striking during the whole course of your life. But if they don't show you any moral, don't put one in. For the moral you put in is likely to be a platitude, or even a falsehood, skimmed from the surface of your consciousness . . . The only moral that is of any value is that which arises inevitably from the whole cast of the author's mind.[8]

Let us not demean art. Let us not bring it down to a means of grabbing people into the kingdom. There will always be those who prefer the stem to the flower, those who believe that painting and poetry exist only that there may be instruction, and love that there may be children, and the sea that there may be warships. But we should not be among that company.

Notes

1. Ed. Murray Watts, *Laughter in Heaven*. MARC Europe, 1985.

2. M. Buxton Foreman, *The Letters of John Keats* (2 volumes). Oxford University Press, 1931.

3. H. Caudwell, *The Creative Impulse in Writing and Painting*. New York: MacMillan, 1953.

4. Burbridge and Watts, *Lightning Sketches*. London: Hodder & Stoughton, 1981.

5. Edward Thomas, *Collected Poems*. London: Faber and Faber, 1920.

6. Michael Frayn, *Donkeys' Years*. London: Metheun, 1977.

7. Watts, ed., *op cit*.

8. C.S. Lewis, *Of Other Worlds*. Bles, 1966.

8

Stage Management

You all but sicken at the shifting scenes . . .
Tennyson, *The Play*

*I*t used to be compulsory in the theater for any aspiring actor to learn first of all about stage management. One can never be certain of the reasoning behind such decisions, but it used to be said—and accurately—that if a would-be actor could not bring himself to perform the most menial tasks in the theater such as sweeping the stage and making the coffee, he was more interested in his own ego than in the success of the play. Or, to put it another way, he who is faithful in small things will be faithful in the greater things.

Certainly, whatever the ostensible reasoning, there is a great deal of sense in coming into acting via stage management, for it teaches those who need to be taught that taking responsibility for the running of a play and the control of a theater company is no easy task. It may lack glamor—though there is little glamor in acting for those who take it seriously—but it calls for just as much skill, commitment, and expertise as any other job in the theater.

Those who enjoy the adulation of the public may look down on the stage management team; those who take their art seriously depend on them. Good ones are above rubies. We should be grateful that there are some for whom stage management is not just a steppingstone toward an acting career but a career in itself, for the craft of a true stage manager is long in the learning and needs a knowledge of many different skills.

There is not the space, nor do I have the expertise, to describe everything a stage manager should know. Those interested in taking on such a job themselves should read some of the technical books available, and a selection of these will be found in the bibliography. This short chapter will simply outline the task and give some general hints about methods and areas of responsibility.

What the Stage Manager Does

The stage manager is in a position roughly analogous to that of a teacher in a school. He is directly responsible to the headmaster (the director) and, by serving the needs of the pupils (the cast), he ensures that education (the play) actually happens. The actual details of his job will vary according to the type of play in production; as will be easily imagined, it is quite a different job to stage an hour-long revue from staging a full-scale musical. But his job will also change depending on how many deputies and assistants he has at his disposal. Somehow or other, the stage manager or his team has to ensure that everything, apart from the acting, gets done at the right time and in the right way. It is really up to him how he does it. But to get an idea of the size of the job, imagine that the director has rehearsed the cast up to performance standard. All they have is a rehearsal space and themselves. What else has to happen in order for the play to be put on? Ask the stage manager.

From the Beginning

Let us trace the stage manager's job through from the original idea of putting on a play right up to the first night. No one person can do all the jobs which will be mentioned and still retain his sanity; some deputizing will have to be done. Nevertheless, for the sake of clarity I shall refer to "the stage manager" rather than "the stage manager or one of his team."

Before the first rehearsal of the play there will be a production meeting which will be attended by everyone involved except the actors. At a typical production meeting, therefore, will be the director, the stage manager, the designer, the costume designer (these last two may be the same person), the lighting designer, the musical director, the choreographer, possibly the author, and an administrator/publicity officer.

At this meeting the director will outline the way he sees the play taking shape, and, after consultation with those responsible for specific areas, some decisions will be made. The designer and costume designer should leave the meeting knowing fairly well what the director wants and how much money they have to spend. Their job is then to produce the designs, for little else can happen before that has been done. The stage manager and the director will work out a schedule of dates for rehearsals—bearing in mind the needs of the musical director and the choreographer—and the publicity officer will be able to start planning the way he is going to advertise the show, what sort of flavor the posters, handouts, programs, etc. should have. Any peculiar needs inherent in the play—a life-size stuffed mammoth or a flock of sheep, perhaps; a hot-air balloon or a musical box in the shape of the Liberty Bell— will be discussed and the author, possibly, shot.

There will be little for the stage manager to do after this initial meeting except, perhaps, to book the rehearsal rooms, make sure the scripts are all available and see that the designs are finished in time for the next meeting. He may be required to check that transport will be available for moving timber and equipment, and to overhaul any stage lighting that will definitely have to be hired and props that need thinking about (the stuffed mammoth, etc.).

The Next Stage

The next production meeting—again, before the first rehearsal—
will be to approve or amend the designs, look at roughs of posters
and handouts, book a time early in rehearsals for the costume
designer (or wardrobe mistress if the designer is not going to make
the costumes himself) to take measurements of the cast.

After this meeting the stage manager will know the design of
the set and be able to mark up the floor for rehearsals. He may be
asked to find some makeshift furniture for the actors to rehearse
with. He may also be asked to find some rehearsal skirts for the
ladies of the cast if the production demands long dresses: it is a
great advantage to rehearse in a long dress if you are supposed to
perform in one.

In most small companies the stage manager is responsible for
constructing any parts of the set that need constructing. This
process should start as soon as possible.

He should then make a list of props that are going to be needed
for the play and set about finding them as soon as possible. He
should then be in attendance at rehearsals so that the director can
communicate to him anything else he needs to do, to add to his list
of props as the actors discover what they need, to mark down the
moves that are set—especially in complicated scenes such as
fights—to make sure the actors are called when they are needed,
to familiarize himself with the way the play is being performed
and, at the same time, to keep a check on how all the different
departments are working together.

A Word about Props

Props can be a very minor affair, or they can provide great complications. In the Riding Lights production of *St. John's Gospel* there

were seven props; in Patrick Garland's production of *Brief Lives* there were literally thousands.

Some props have to be made. Famous oil-paintings, twelfth-century manuscripts, and sundry objects familiar enough on an Elizabethan scholar's desk, for instance, are not lying around for the taking. But it is surprising how often a modern object, after a little tatting up, will pass muster even from the first row of seats. Indeed, a great deal of modern kitchenware is very similar to that used in New Testament times, and a sensible stage manager will capitalize on that. The making of good props is an art in itself, and, again, I refer the reader to the bibliography for books dealing with the subject.

But, if you have not already tried, you may be surprised at the willingness of local retailers and even museums to lend objects to theater companies. You may need to use a bit of charm; you may need, sometimes, to write to the head office of larger firms, but in return for an acknowledgment in the program or two complimentary tickets for the first night, most shops will be reasonably happy to lend something for a week or so. Remember that it will make your job easier in the future if, having promised to return a prop by a particular date, you actually do so. Once you have established yourself as untrustworthy, you are not going to be able to borrow things so easily in the future. Keep a list of what you have borrowed, where you have borrowed it from, when it has to be returned, and any deposit or guarantee you have been asked to make.

It is wise to make any such lists in a hardback book which is too big to lose. This will be a useful record of what was needed for the show, and can be referred to by future stage managers who may want to know which companies were willing to lend to you and under what conditions. Lists kept on scrappy pieces of paper stuffed into a back pocket have a way of going through the washing machine without drawing attention to themselves, or taking themselves off for a scamper down the street in blustery wind.

One Stage Further

Suppose we are now well into rehearsals, the props have been gathered or are in the process of construction, the set is being painted, the costumes are almost finished, and the posters are appearing around town as well as advertisements in the newspaper and interviews or items on the local radio (whenever that is possible). This might be a good time for the stage manager to record any music or sound effects that the director requires. Recordings of sound effects can be bought, but if there is a local radio station or a professional theater, the chances are that they will have a library of sound effects which they will be happy to lend—again, in return for an acknowledgment. The local record library should also be able to obtain them for you if necessary.

Do not use a cassette for playing sound effects: it is quite impossible, even in full daylight (let alone semi-darkness), to tell whereabouts you are on the tape, and there is nothing more calculated to destroy the whole show than to cue a bomb exploding and hear a baby crying, or to hear the leading man say, "I'll put on some Bach," and get a mastiff howling in the distance.

There is a simple and foolproof way to construct a sound-tape. Record the first cue after the first strip of leader-tape, as normal. If it is a simple cue which has a definite time-span, such a glass being smashed or a car door closing, then that is what you record and there is no problem. If, however, it is a cue that has to last in the background until a certain point in the play—background party noise, a television in the next room, distant gunfire, etc.—then work out roughly how long it is liable to last and record quite a lot more than you need, just in case the scene goes particularly slowly, or in case one of the actors forgets. At the end of that cue, insert a strip of leader-tape *of a different color* from the last. Then record the next cue. Follow that with leader-tape, again of a different color, and so on until all the cues are on tape and separated by a longish piece of leader-tape each time.

Now, during the performance, as each cue finishes or fades out, you can wind on to the next cue. The leader-tape will show you when it is about to appear. The different colors are just a double check for you that you have wound on to the correct cue. This will be absolutely necessary for you if, for instance, the actors should lose their heads and miss out half a page of the play which contains a cue. You can always tell from the color of the leader what sound is about to come.

Wind through the leader-tape to the point where it joins the magnetic tape. Stop the tape so that the join is right on the playing head. Then, when you press the button, the cue will come immediately.

If incidental music is needed during scene-changes or blackouts, this can be on a separate cassette since it will not really matter where you start it and finish it. Keep it on a separate machine from your sound-effect tape, or you can get into terrible difficulties. Do not be tempted to put the incidental music on the sound-cue tape and treat it like a kind of extra sound cue, for the incidental music will have to be of an indefinite length, and what will happen if you have to fade the music and go straight into a sound effect? You will not be able to do it, of course, except by an amazing coincidence.

When the cue-tape has been made up, label it, put it into a box, and mark the box with the name of the show. Remember, too, that if you are using music from a commercial recording, you will have to get permission and pay a nominal fee.

The Last Stage

The technical rehearsal is now approaching. Everything is ready—set, props, costumes, equipment. The next thing to do is light the show and make up the prompt-copy of the script.

The lighting is the last, most magical piece of the jigsaw. If, as stage manager, you are also supposed to be in charge of the lighting, then do not learn it from this book; refer to the books men-

tioned in the bibliography and prepare yourself for an arduous
course of study. Lighting is not just a matter of making sure things
can be seen and being able to change a plug. Lighting a production
is as skilled a job as directing it or acting in it; being an electrician
is no qualification, though it is a first step. The apparent simplicity
of lighting is the result of great complexity. Many a production has
been lifted by a skilled lighting designer from the merely good to
the inspirational.

Here, for I can do no more, I shall outline the very basic principles and techniques which lie behind the art of stage lighting.
Lighting must do several things, sometimes simultaneously: it
must allow the action to be seen, it must direct the audience's
attention, it must make individuals or areas stand out in relation
to the rest of the scene, and it must be able to create special effects
such as fire, moonlight, water, and so forth.

To achieve these effects the lighting designer can do any of the
following:

He can decide to use either floods or spots.
He can vary the light's intensity by the use of dimmers.
He can color the light with filters.
He can vary the angle at which the light falls.
He can vary the throw, the shape, and the size of the beam.

Floods are lanterns which give a wide throw or wash of light. Spots
have a reflector behind a bulb and a lens in front so the light can be
focused very sharply. The profile spot has a hard edge to its beam
of light, while the fresnel spot has a softer edge and can be fitted
with a set of shutters called barndoors to shape the beam. Thus,
floods can never be used in order to define areas, for their throw is
too wide; nor can they be used from a distance, or they will light
areas that should remain dark. They are good for giving an overall

general cover, either from stands in the wings or ganged together on battens hung above the stage area.

When light needs to be defined, spotlights are used.

The intensity of the light depends on factors other than its intrinsic brightness as controlled through a dimmer. The color and reflectiveness of the surface which is lit is an important factor, as is the color of the light itself, its distance from the object (and the spectator), and its relation to the other lights. One small lamp on a dark stage can look warm and bright, but two huge floods trying to cover a whole stage will look wan and shadowy by themselves.

Remember that light does not work in the same way as colors from a paint box. If you place a red, a green, and a blue filter in front of a lantern, no light will pass through. If, however, you shine a red lantern plus a green lantern plus a blue lantern onto the same white surface, the effect will be of white light.

The most difficult thing to obtain with limited resources is what is usually demanded by the director: an even spread of light across the whole stage. It is disturbing for the audience when actors moving across the stage walk through holes of darkness or shadow, or when the actors' shadows fall on the faces of other actors. One can achieve a general lighting by lighting *separate* but *overlapping* areas of the stage. In this way individual areas can be lit independently and variations of intensity can be obtained over the whole stage space. Each area should be lit by a pair of spots from different sides of the auditorium, each at an angle of about 45 degrees to the vertical and to the horizontal. If the performance is in the round, four spots will have to be used so that an actor is lit from every side.

Key lighting or motivational lighting is the lighting which sets the mood for the scene by showing light of a particular quality from a particular source. It might be morning light streaming through french windows into a living room; light from a group of candles illuminating the faces of three people sitting around a table, or the harsh, cold light of a hospital ward on a winter afternoon. Once the right mood has been caught by these key lights, it will be a fairly simple task to introduce visibility into other areas by "cheating" up a few subtle spots.

A *special* is a light which is used for one particular purpose or effect apart from the purposes already mentioned. It might be a single overhead spot to pick out one actor at a dramatic point, a light from a window, or follow-spot; anything, in fact, that will not be used in the plotting of the rest of the lighting scheme.

Special effects can be obtained by the use of gobos, which are a sort of stencil cut out in metal and slipped in front of the light with the filter. These can give the impression of a window pattern being thrown on a floor, for instance, or a pattern of light falling through leaves in a forest. Used subtly they can be very atmospheric. You *can* make your own out of cardboard, but be careful it does not stay in too long and catch fire; lanterns can generate an amazing amount of heat.

We have hardly scratched the surface of stage lighting, but to go any further would be to write a whole book. Fortunately this has been done, and we can proceed to discussing and describing that most important manual, the prompt copy.

The basis of the prompt copy is formed by sticking each page of the script into a much larger notebook, or onto large sheets of paper that can be put into a ring file in order to make up a book. Thus, when the book is opened the script will appear on the right-hand page, and the left-hand page will be blank. But not for long.

On this left-hand page will be noted all the moves that have been set in rehearsal and all the cues which have to be given to the person in charge of the sound, plus all the calls to the actors in their dressing rooms, and any reminders of other things that have to be done during the show, from waiting off stage with a change of clothes for one of the actors, to turning on the coffeepot for the intermission.

This may not be applicable to small groups who seldom perform in a well-equipped theater, but I shall describe the process because the main point of it is precision and discipline. This applies to any group, and groups can adapt or simplify this process as is most suitable for them.

The stage manager's job, during the performance, is to keep in touch with whoever is operating the lights and the sound and warn him when a cue is approaching and precisely when it actually has to happen. The easiest way to do this is to mark every cue with a green line stretching from the exact point in the script when it takes place, across to the blank page. This is called the GO, and is marked as such, in green, along with the number of the cue. The first cue is number 1, the second number 2, and so on. Lighting cues are designated LX, for short, and sound cues, S.

So, when the first lighting change takes place, the script will be marked with a green line against which is written LXQ 1 GO. When the first sound cue comes it will be marked in the same way but with SQ 1 GO.

The warning or *stand by* for each cue should probably come about a quarter of a page before the cue itself so that the technician is prepared. This is marked in a similar way but with a *red* line and STAND BY LXQ 14, or STAND BY SQ 7, and so on.

If there are a number of cues on the same page, the warning period will have to be shorter, or in a kind of omnibus edition such as STAND BY LXQ's 3, 4, and 4a. The designation 4a probably means that after all the cues were worked out the director decided to make a small change. It is better to add a cue 4a than to go through the whole book changing every number.

Even if the stage manager is doing the sound or the lighting himself, it is necessary to have the script marked up like this so that mistakes are reduced to a minimum. Following is a specimen page of a prompt copy. It is a genuine one from the first page of my pantomime *Jack and the Beanstalk* which was performed at Theatr

<u>STAND BY</u>
   LXQ1 + SQ1
   TABS

<u>AFTER CLEARANCE</u>
   H/L, TABWARMERS GO
   TABS GO
   LXQ1 GO
   SQ1 GO

CALL: MR. BURNS, MR. BAGLEY

      <u>STAND BY</u>
   LXQ2
   SQ1A

Juggler on U.S.L.
   Flys Q1

Jack X D.S.L.
   LXQ2 GO

   Flys Q1 GO)
   SQ1A GO }

      <u>STAND BY</u>
   LXQ's 2A. 3. 4,
   SQ 2

Str & G on.
     ON PIANO RUN
   LXQ 2A GO

   LXQ3 GO
   SQ2 GO
   (PAUSE)
   LXQ4 GO

CALL WARDROBE TO ASSIST MR. BAGLEY

      <u>STAND BY</u>
   LXQ's 5, 6. 7. 7a, 8a, 9
   SQ's 3, 3a. 5, 5a, 5b, 7, 7a
   FLASHES

     SQ3 GO

Clwyd. The calls to actors are put through on an internal speaker system to warn actors to stand by ready for their next entrance.

Running the Show

The stage manager has to ensure that every member of the cast is in the theater by the half. Though the expression "the half" is short for "the half hour before curtain up" it actually means thirty-five minutes before the curtain goes up. Every call to the dressing rooms is given five minutes before the time implied in the actual call. The quarter is called twenty minutes before curtain up, the five is called ten minutes before curtain up, and the call for beginners is made five minutes before curtain up. This is not because actors have to be treated as if they were daft or unreliable, it is simply a hangover from the times when the calls were made in person by a call-boy. He obviously couldn't call at every dressing room at the same time, so he went first to the lowest of the low, the chorus in the dressing rooms at the top of the building and worked his way down to the star dressing room on the ground floor nearest the stage. In order to call the star exactly on the half hour, he had to start five minutes early at the top. The tradition has stuck, and it is no bad thing for the actors to assemble in the wings and get the flavor of the performance during the last few minutes.

The stage manager will have been in touch with the front-of-house manager during the half hour before curtain up, checking that the audience is coming in steadily and not all waiting until the last minute. By keeping in touch and not just starting the performance willy-nilly at seven-thirty, the odd latecomer or delayed party can be accommodated.

Before the half, the stage manager will have checked that everything that should be set on stage actually has been set, and so, if he has any sense, will each of the actors. Actors will also have checked their personal props—that is, props which they bring on themselves and for which the stage manager has no responsibility—things such as cigarettes, notebooks, shopping bags.

When all is ready, the houselights will be cued to fade, any music will be cued to start, and the tabwarmers (lights shining on the curtain) brought in. The tabs (front curtains) will be cued to go (up), and the show will be underway.

The stage manager's job is now to sit and follow the whole show in the script and give all the stand-bys and cues to whoever requires them.

Within this framework, of course, there can be and will be almost infinite variation, but it must always be remembered that, once the show is running, the stage manager is in command; he has taken the place of the director and has responsibility for everything that happens.

9

Getting It Right

Only the ephemeral is of lasting value.
                                        Ionesco, *Improvisation*

*T*heater is an ephemeral art. Once gone, it has gone for good. You can treasure a book or a painting and look at it again and again: it will never change. Every performance of a piece of music or of a play is a unique experience. We need to give it the best start possible by framing it attractively, by advertising it well, and by putting people into an attitude of mind in which they are prepared for an enjoyable experience.

Sir Thomas Beecham, in a remark that is unduly cynical even for him, once said that if an orchestra starts together and finishes together it doesn't matter very much what goes on in between. Whether it is a welcome truth or not, an average performance of a play can be greatly enhanced and made much more enjoyable by the conditions under which the audience is expected to watch it. Bring three hundred people late into a dank, unattractive, drafty hall after they have been left standing in the drizzle while the front-of-house manager goes back home for the key he forgot, issue them a blurred page of badly-typed paper, sit them on hard, creaky chairs, give some of them (there isn't enough for all of them) a cup of tepid, supermarket, instant coffee with lumpy powdered milk during the intermission, and the show has got to be an absolute stunner to get them to respond.

Of course, if the only place you have in which you can perform is bleak and unattractive, you cannot turn it into a posh theater overnight; but you can make sure that the doors are open exactly when they should be, you can reduce the bleakness with subtle lighting, heating, and plenty of greenery, and you can have a cheerful, brisk, friendly person to greet them and charm them to their seats.

If you conceive it as "an occasion" and do your best to make it so, the chances are that the audience will also remember it as an occasion. For a start, the manager could wear a dinner jacket or a suit, at least. The ushers, even if they are pressed volunteers and different every night, should know something about the company and the production so that they can answer interested questions.

Publicity

We touched on this subject in discussing the production meeting. If there is any money available, it is well spent on good posters, handouts, and programs. These are not cheap, but it is worth an exploratory interview or two to see if any local firm would sponsor this side of the production. Perhaps in your congregation there is a businessman who would support the performance. Be sure that they will never *offer* to do so, but they might be delighted to be asked.

Try to find a design concept that will do for poster, handout, and program. Give your publicity continuity or at least find a motif that can be repeated and used as a unifying factor. Ill-designed, hasty, makeshift publicity will reflect on the play; the cleaner and more professional it looks, the more people will take you seriously.

With a bit of forethought, the program can actually make money. A properly produced, glossy, well-printed program will cost something to produce, but if it is good enough, advertisers might be persuaded to pay for an advertisement in it which will help offset the cost. You will be able to charge a fair price for such an article, whereas a plain sheet of paper is not worth anything.

The best publicity you will ever have is the talent of the cast and the company, so if you are planning to produce another play in the future, advertise it now to those who are coming. Mention it in the program, blazon it in the foyer, give people handouts about it as they leave. Such publicity will never be wasted; the people you are talking to are, after all, theater-goers or they would not be there.

Photographs

Photographs are extremely attractive on display in a foyer. Good photographs make the production look exciting and interesting, and a well-arranged exhibition of photographs and posters can be a very impressive way of welcoming the audience into the theater. With this in mind, don't get someone's uncle who was given a Polaroid for Christmas to take the pictures. Hire a professional, and the results will pay for themselves.

Special photo-calls might have to be arranged. The press, for some reason, always like to pose their photographs without reference to the director or to the meaning of the play. If they see a pretty girl or an interesting costume, they will pose them together, photograph them, and print an inane picture in the newspaper—beautifully composed, superbly developed and printed, but quite empty.

The best way to get good photographs is to employ an experienced stage photographer and then do a complete dress rehearsal while he wanders about among the actors with his cameras, photographing what he finds interesting. The pictures then have both his thought and the actors' thought behind them, and something really worthwhile results.

The Production Schedule

To conclude this section, here is a quick checklist of all the jobs to be done from the moment you decide on a play until the first night. What jobs are done by whom will depend on the size of the company from which you can draw, but somehow they have all got to be done.

1. Obtain the performance rights for the play. The necessary address will be in the script if it is published. If it is not published, obtain the author's permission.

2. Find a suitable theater or hall in which to perform, and make sure it is available for the last two or three days of rehearsal and however long it will take you to rig the lights and erect the set. Make sure that it has a license for public performances.

3. Choose your production team and have the first production meeting.

4. Plan your budget. Income will be from tickets, programs, refreshments, and any sponsorship you can raise. Outgoings will be on fees, materials, and hiring of equipment, on publicity, telephone and mailing, and buying of sufficient scripts.

5. Check the blackout and lighting of the theater. There should be an emergency lighting system on a different circuit from the main lights. If there is not, you will have to provide one. It can be run off a car battery, but it is legally necessary.

6. Make sure everything you use is fireproofed. Get the local fire officer in for advice and approval before you go ahead with the show. He has the power to stop it if he wants to.

7. Plan the production schedule so that set, costumes, PA, props, and any other equipment are all there when they are required.

8. Make sure tickets and programs are printed in good time.

9. Book a photographer for the first dress rehearsal, and be sure he knows how quickly you will need the finished photographs.

10. Send complimentary tickets to anybody who has helped you or to anybody you will be asking to help you during the next production.

11. Prepare what publicity you can for the next production so that it is available to be seen by the audience for this one.

12. Enlist smart, charming, willing helpers for front-of-house work.

This is a list only of the technical schedule to be followed; the artistic side will continue concurrently with all these tasks. If they "get it right" as well, you should have a success on your hands.

Afterword

Our revels now are ended. These our actors,
As I foretold you, were all spirits, and
Are melted into air, into thin air . . .

Shakespeare, *The Tempest*

*B*ecause I have been writing for Christians I have tried not to over-spiritualize this book. We all know what we believe, why we believe it, and how it affects our lives. This book has been simply an answer to the question, "How do we do it?" and that, in itself, does not imply anything spiritual at all. It is a method, and it is a method which has to be learned whether one is a believer or not. Sometimes the matter of belief does enter into the content and into the way in which we work, and in those cases I have tried to show how and why a Christian perspective is worked out.

Christianity, however, is the context in which we live and move and have our being, and our spiritual lives do impinge on our artistic lives; but possibly not in the way that many people think. If I were not a Christian I would still be an artist. Whether I would be a worse one I find it very difficult to say. The question really is, "Worse in whose eyes?" And the only sensible answer to that is, "In God's eyes." For, apart from my standing in the sight of God, there is very little that is different about me from the time when I was not a Christian. I have the same talent, the same background, the same education, the same face, the same nervous system, the same upbringing, the same grasp of the language, and the same intelligence. What makes me an artist, in other words, is not the same thing as what makes me a Christian, though the two do overlap.

This is why we must be aware of the assumption that Christian artists are, *ipso facto*, better than pagan artists. God does not suddenly confer talents upon those who turn to him.

I mention this because I believe there is a great confusion in people's minds between moral goodness and goodness at something—which we discussed in Chapter 1 under the heading "Sacred and Secular"—and between talents and spiritual gifts.

Now the Bible is quite specific in its teaching about spiritual gifts. We are told "earnestly" to "desire" the higher gifts and, if we do, we will be given them. And these gifts *are* given to people—gifts of discernment and prophecy and healing. They do not belong to the individual, like the color of his hair or the sharpness of his elbows; they are given as and when they are needed.

I believe talents are gifts of a different sort. They are given once and for all, and we are to make the most of them. They do belong to us in as much as they are part of our personality, of our mental and physical make-up, and yet, of course, they are still gifts from God. But I believe that to pray for this kind of gift is to be disappointed. Prayer isn't magic. I really do not believe that any amount of prayer tonight will make me able to play the Elgar Cello Concerto tomorrow.

It's worth remembering the wise words attributed to St. Irenaus:

Work as if everything depended on you;
Pray as if everything depended on God.

To be a Christian is to ally yourself with the Truth behind the universe. It is not to be a receiver but a giver, not to be constantly waiting for God to give you what you want but to use what he has given you, not to seek always for encouragement but for truth.

Some of the things I have said or implied in this book may have been discouraging to many people; I do not mind that. Indeed, I think it is necessary—especially in the area of the arts which all too easily encourage glibness and self-glorification at the expense of hard work and commitment—to throw down a challenge to Christians, a challenge which asks, "Are you called to this work by nature, talent, and commitment? Are you doing it to glorify God—however personally hurtful it may be—or just jumping on a bandwagon? Are you following the fashion or breaking new ground? Is this the talent that God has given you, or are you trying to avoid using the one he really *has* given you?"

The trouble with theater is that, yes, one can do it in the right spirit, one can offer it to God in all sincerity, one can do it for his glory, but in the end you have to impress the audience *too*, or it doesn't work. We wouldn't think much of a fisherman who said he fished for God's glory but never caught anything, or a gardener called to his work by God but never able to grow anything. And yet in the arts, excruciatingly bad poems, sketches, and songs are allowed, even encouraged, if they are well meant. I wonder if the same encouragement would be offered me if I approached an ill member of the congregation with a scalpel in my unpracticed hand and said, "It's all right—I've prayed about it . . ."

We must decide where we stand. If the arts are a mere frill, then let's not bother with them at all—they're not worth it. If they are important let us recognize the fact and treat them as if they are.

I have a great deal of sympathy, for instance, with members of the congregation who do not want to see drama in their church. I would take issue with them if they claimed that theater was intrinsically un-Christian or devilish, but I cannot quarrel with them if they simply do not like it or cannot see the point of it during worship. I sometimes cringe to hear arrogant young members of drama groups moaning about the fuddy-duddies who don't like them to perform sketches during the services. The drama group thinks it is a good idea, so everyone else is wrong. One can often understand why they are not always welcome in church.

Sometimes a piece of theater can hit the nail on the head and render fresh and vivid a concept which a preacher might take half an hour to clarify. On the other hand liturgy is, in essence, reconciliation and drama is, in essence, conflict; they do not always mix well. Worship is not a spectator sport; drama depends on its being watched. If your work is that powerful, it won't hurt it to be taken out of church and into the church hall or school or theater where it can be attended to without preconceptions and barriers being raised. We all need to stand up for what we believe in, but we need graciousness, too, and an understanding of other people's tastes and fears.

I believe in theater and the arts; I believe in them passionately. I believe that for many people they are the means, above all other, whereby the Spirit of God can communicate himself to them. But that is why I also believe that they should be taken seriously, studied, worked at, and respected.

The amateur has always this advantage over the professional, that whatever he does he does for love and nothing else. He never *need* do anything; he is not bound to use his love to earn a living, to boil a pot or to please an employer. He can create, polish, and perfect with no deadline hanging over him. He can do it for the sheer joy of doing it. I offer this book in the hope that it will excite him, stimulate him, and lead him to deepen and enrich that joy.

Appendix

Some sketches. They are not strictly necessary to the book, but they may help to illustrate some of the points I have been making about parody and satire.

We begin with what is little more than a dramatized joke which I have then parodied in the styles of two of the most important dramatists of the twentieth century, Pinter and Brecht. It might be an interesting exercise to write your own version of *The Fiddle* in the style of other writers. Remember that the material dictates the style to quite a large extent. It would be hard to do a version of this particular sketch in the style of, say, Ayckbourn or Coward. One might, however, try Wesker, Simpson, Ionesco, Orton, Synge, Agatha Christie, or Enid Blyton. Remember, too, that the parody must work as a sketch which is amusing in its own right; there should be enough in it to entertain someone who has no idea that it is a parody.

Prose and Amateurs was written at the time of the 1964 Olympic Games when dozens of countries withdrew from participation and turned the whole thing into an anti-climax, making the media coverage look slightly overblown and silly. It is an example of the one-thing-in-terms-of-another sketch, a genre of which I am very fond.

I Mean to Say is simply satire. Fortunately for actors and unfortunately for the country it is a sketch that will probably never be out-of-date. I have always been fascinated by the sort of summit talks which need an interpreter: how accurate is the interpretation? How can the American President be absolutely sure that what he has said to the Soviet leaders has been truthfully transmitted by the interpreter? Imagine the things that could go wrong! It was a kind of extension of this idea allied with the fact that politicians and what one might term "para-politicians" hardly ever say what they actually mean anyway, that led to this sketch.

Sharing the Joke is a monologue which I have specifically referred to earlier in the book. I thought it would be helpful to reproduce the whole of it here.

The Fiddle

A TRAMP *stands at the corner of the street. At his feet is a violin in a case. He shivers and, with numb fingers, takes out the violin, puts down his cap, and begins to play. A haunting melancholy little tune. He puts the violin away carefully and inspects the cap. Nothing. With infinite sadness he picks up the case and crosses the stage. Cross fade into a dingy shop. The bell on the door tinkles as the* TRAMP *enters. Nobody comes. Then a* PAWNBROKER *comes out from the back of the shop. He is cunning-looking. He wears a greasy, eggstained suit.*

Pawnbroker:	Well? *(The* TRAMP *is struggling inwardly)* Come on, squire, it's dark and it's cold, and I want to get home for me supper. If you've got anything to sell let's see it.
Tramp:	*(Taking out the violin lovingly)* I don't want 'er to go, but I gotter eat, haven't I? She's . . . well, she's all I got left now; I got nothin' . . . nothin'.
Pawnbroker:	*(Snatching violin roughly)* Let's have a look . . .
Tramp:	Careful. *(Awkwardly)* I know she ain't much but—you know how it is. It'll break my 'eart ter part with 'er.
Pawnbroker:	*(Unmoved)* All right, all right. Stay here a minute. *(He goes through an imaginary curtain into an ante-room and glances condescendingly at the violin. Glances inside; freezes; looks again. His whole body stiffens, and his eyes glint. He grabs a tome, blows off the dust, and flaps through the pages with intense excitement)* St . . . St . . . Strad . . . where are we? . . . Strad . . . Stradivarius! *(He checks again inside the violin and gives a short, almost panic-stricken laugh.*

*He reads the entry in the book swiftly and in a
mutter. We only catch a word here and there)*
Stradivarius . . . blah blah blah . . . Cremona
violins by the master of . . . blah blah blah . . .
end of the century . . . blah blah blah . . .
1682 . . . blah blah . . . but has never been discovered!! *(He looks up, overwhelmed)*
Stradivarius! 1682!! *(Then he checks himself)*
It's a fake. *(Looks back at book again)* Fakes . . .
fakes . . . blah . . . blah . . . at the bottom of
the scroll. *(He checks the violin and is almost beside himself. Pulls himself together and goes back
into the shop with a forced air of nonchalance)*
Yeah . . . well, I don't know. I *might* be able to
get rid of it, but, I mean—it's not like a
watch, is it? Or a bit of china.

Tramp: *(Looking disappointed)* No . . . well. No, all
             right . . .
             *(He goes to take back the violin and the pawn-
             broker hastily becomes more flexible)*

Pawnbroker: Look, I'll tell you what. I'm a fair man. I'll give
             you thirty bucks for it.

Tramp: *(He is undecided)* Thirty bucks . . .

Pawnbroker: All right, then. It *has* got a case. Forty dollars
             and that's as far as I can go.

Tramp: *(Fingering the case lovingly)* Well . . . yer see . . .
             I'd hoped for a bit more than that . . .

Pawnbroker: Oh, had you indeed! Huh—like how much, for
             instance?

Tramp: Well . . . I mean . . . like—about five hundred
             and eighty-seven thousand three hundred
             and twelve.

                        Blackout

The Fiddle (after Harold Pinter)

A TRAMP *stands, blowing into his hands, one the corner of a street. There is a violin case at his feet. Enter* MAN. *He is dressed neatly in a suit and a pale raincoat. He stops. The* TRAMP *does not see him. He looks at the* TRAMP *for a long time. He walks round him. The* TRAMP *bends towards the violin case but freezes as the* MAN *stops and turns.*

Tramp:	*(Nervously)* What d'you want?
Man:	*(Very much in command)* I'd like an anchovy. I'm very partial to anchovies. You wouldn't have such a thing as an anchovy about you, would you? No. You don't look the sort to carry anchovies. I've got a taste for anchovies. A penchant. *(He leans towards the* TRAMP *and brings out a cigarette case)* Cigarette? *(The* TRAMP *hesitates)* I asked if you would like a cigarette. *(As the* TRAMP *goes to take one, he snaps the case shut and shouts)* I know what's going through your sullied little mind! If I'm affluent enough to own a cigarette case, why don't I carry anchovies? *(His voice has dropped during this speech. He is suddenly violent again)* What do you know about anchovies, you dirty old scruff!
Tramp:	I haven't eaten for two days.
Man:	Force yourself!
Tramp:	If I had a few pounds . . .
Man:	Don't you try it on with me! I'm not affluent. *(They look at each other)* Go on, now. *(Gently)* There's a good boy. *(He goes swiftly. The* TRAMP *picks up the violin case and goes into*

the shop. When the pawnbroker appears, it is the
MAN. *No raincoat, jeans, jacket and sunglasses)*

Man: Yes?

Tramp: It's me.

Man: Come in. How are you?

Tramp: I'm fine.

Man: He's in.

Tramp: What do you mean "he's in"?

Man: He's gone in.

Tramp: Gone in where?

Man: His room.

Tramp: His room?

Man: Gone into his room?

Tramp: So, he's in there.

Man: I wanted to say—I was a bit rude. I wanted to apologize.

Tramp: You weren't rude.

Man: *(Taking violin case)* I'll take this. I'd ask you to sit down and relax. Cross your legs. Take things easy. But it's hardly your place.

Man: *(goes into the back of the shop and opens violin case. Takes out a tin of anchovies. Looks carefully into the case.)* Stradivarius. It's a name I know. *(Whispers loudly off)* It's come! It's a Stradivarius. What? *(Stuffs anchovies into pocket)* No. No anchovies. *(Comes back into the shop with the violin)* It'll do. I'll give you five pounds for it.

Tramp: Is that the arrangement?

Man: That's it?

Tramp: Five pounds.

Man: That's expensive for firewood. *(Pause)*

Tramp: If that's the arrangement . . .

Man: Oh yes. You can take my word for it.

Tramp: I'll need a receipt.

Man: (*Humiliating him*) You'll need a receipt? What would a man in your position do with a receipt? What benefit would a receipt be to you? Can you see the advantage of a receipt? (*Suddenly charming*) I'll get you one. (*He goes. While he is gone the* TRAMP *opens the violin case and smashes the violin to matchwood. He steps back. The* MAN *returns. Sees the wreck of the violin. He lifts his eyes. They meet those of the* TRAMP *and hold them. There is a long pause*)

Tramp: It's ready for the fire now. (*Pause*) It's quite ready. (*They look at each other as the lights slowly fade*)

The Fiddle (after Berthold Brecht)

Narrator: At the end of the day we crossed the border and came to a village where we were to distribute our leaflets. There was no rice in the village and the people were starving, so we talked to them about the party and told them how they were being exploited. Many of the workers were sympathetic to our cause, but some refused to listen, holding their stomachs and groaning.

Tramp: I am a worker. I have not eaten for three days. The factory-owners have piled up rice in their warehouses so that rice is scarce and too expensive. There is no work for me, so I stand at the side of the road and play music.

Owner: I am a factory-owner. I have plenty of rice. I am going to keep it in my warehouse beside the river for a long time and its value will rise. I have no ear for music. I will recite to you my poem.

> You can only help yourself and
> your brothers by squashing others.
> Why is it? I do not know.
> Eat rice, you dogs, eat rice.
> A little is enough and I've got
> plenty.
> That is why I am full and others are
> empty.

Listen to me. If you will stop playing your instrument and give it to me I will give you rice.

Tramp: How much rice will you give me?

Owner: A bushel.

Tramp: What is that in platefuls?
           A governor was asked, "What is needed
           So that the crops will not fail in this
           drought?"
           He replied, "If the people believe
           That the crops will fail, they may water
           them
           With their tears."
           Here is my instrument. I will gladly give it to
           you for food.

Narrator: The factory-owner took the instrument. Seeing
           that it was made by a famous craftsman he
           gave the worker forty bushels of rice.
           Enough to last him for many years.

Owner: See how clever I am. For only forty bushels of
           rice I have procured a rare instrument made
           by a famous craftsman. It will be enough to
           buy me ten thousand bushels of rice.

Tramp: See how the capitalist is trodden underfoot. Now
           I have forty bushels of rice by the simple ex-
           pedient of scribbling "Stradivarius" inside
           my instrument.

Both: You can only help yourself and your brothers.
           By cheating others. Why is it? I do not know.

Prose and Amateurs

One: Welcome to this special edition of Sportsland
where the news is that the first medals in this
year's Olympics have been won, and already a
new World Record has been set! The medals, of
course, are for the very first event—the race for
Official Withdrawal from the Games. You'll
remember that the previous record was held by
the Americans for their withdrawal from the
Moscow Olympics. Let's just remind ourselves
of that speech, because it was that that set the
standard.

American V/O: It is after a great deal of discussion and debate
that the United States of America has regret-
fully found it necessary to make the decision
to withdraw their athletes from the Olympic
Games to be held in Moscow this year.

One: That was the speech, and, my word, what a
standard it set: 14.35 seconds. David, did you
think that would ever be beaten?

Two: It was a good speech, David; well-paced, well
delivered, but I think he just lost concentration toward the end. He was probably a bit
tense; there's always a lot of nervousness on
big occasions like this. I think you'll find he
began to slow down as soon as he got in
sight of the period. He's got through . . .

One: Er . . . sorry, er . . . sorry to interrupt you there,
David, but let's just listen to it again in slow
motion. The last stretch coming up to the
punctuation.

American V/O:	. . . from the Olympic Games to be held . . . in
Slowed down:	. . . Moscow . . . this . . . yeeeeaaarr.
Two:	Yes, you could hear it quite clearly there on the replay.
One:	It's after the word "held," isn't it? Do you think the double consonant is giving him trouble?
Two:	I think Americans have always found it difficult to put more than two or three words together and make any sense, David. They're unbeatable over short distances—monosyllables, wisecracks, but they can't seem to get their sentences together.
One:	Well today, as we know, that record was beaten, and by an amazing 3.12 seconds. And here's how it was done:
Russian V/O:	We are dissatisfied both with the security and with the commercialization of the Olympic Games; the Soviet Union therefore announces its intention to withdraw its athletes.
One:	David?
Two:	Well, what can you say, David? A tremendous performance from the Russian lad. He doesn't put a foot wrong—and you've got to remember that he's talking in an unfamiliar language, he hasn't really had time to acclimatize himself to the syntax.
One:	Quite remarkable.
Two:	He was incisive, positive; no hesitation at all. Two coordinate main clauses, and bang!—he's through the period. It was a great statement.
One:	He went through that semi-colon as if it wasn't there!
Two:	That's right, David.

One: Well, the silver and bronze medals went to
          Rumania and Czechoslovakia; there were a
          few disqualifications for not using full sen-
          tences. Amazingly enough, all the times
          were inside the American record of 14.35
          which is quite staggering. Why do you think
          this is, David?

Two: Training, David.

One: Is that all it is?

Two: Training and temperament, David. The Russians
          have got a great track-record of writers and
          speakers who use the language consistently
          well—Tolstoy, Pushkin, Chekov—and these
          lads are in that tradition. They can put their
          clauses together and they're unbeatable over
          long distances.

One: *War and Peace, Anna Karenina . . . ?*

Two: That's right, and any one of the Three Sisters
          would hit the tape before even the First of
          the Mohicans.

One: Thank you, David. That's all for now. Later this
          evening in a Sportsland special, I'll be talk-
          ing to David Lodge about his definitive
          studies of relay-racing—"How Far Can You
          Go" and "Changing Places"; we'll be discuss-
          ing Structuralism in the 100 meter hurdles,
          and the influence of Zola on British Ath-
          letics. Good night.

                    Music and fade

I Mean to Say

Interviewer:	Good evening and welcome to *Stalemate*, the magazine program that brings you the latest on what people are saying and what they really think. This week's discussion is between Mr. Dan Spiller, representing the Trade Unions.
Dan:	Good evening.
Interviewer:	And the President of the United States.
Mr. President:	Thank you. I'm glad to have this opportunity of talking to Dan, and of course to the millions of viewers at home, and getting some of the issues of the moment clarified right here and now; of putting them before the public in black and white, straight down the line, without fear or favor.
Interviewer:	He says he's ready to dodge any issue you raise.
Dan:	With respect, Mr. President . . .
Interviewer:	With no respect, Mr. President . . .
Dan:	We want a fair, equitable settlement with room for negotiation on both sides.
Interviewer:	He says he's going to rip you off for everything you've got.
Dan:	The important thing for all unions at this stage is solidarity.
Interviewer:	If the country's going to be crippled anyway, he's going to put the boot in, too.
Dan:	It may mean industrial action.
Interviewer:	It may mean industrial inaction
Mr. President:	Dan, we need to understand one another.
Interviewer:	Shut up and listen to me.
Mr. President:	What is needed is a period of stability—time to take stock and look at the situation objectively,

so that we can move forward together into a
new phase of cooperation which will benefit
both the government and the TUC.

Interviewer: He says he doesn't know what to do, but give
him time and he'll make something up.

Dan: I've given this matter a lot of thought, and what
I think is this . . .

Interviewer: What he's been told to say is this . . .

Dan: What are you going to do about it?

Interviewer: What are you going to do about it?

Mr. President: We in the government have made our position
clear on this, and there is no question of our
going back on the promises we made to the
electorate in May.

Interviewer: Can't remember.

Dan: We want a fair wage for a fair week's work.

Interviewer: He wants jam on it.

Mr. President: I think you're forgetting the Stage 2 Proposals
which we made in consultation with both
unions and management.

Interviewer: Liar.

Dan: I'm not forgetting the Stage 2 Proposals, but
there's more at stake here than simply a
political decision.

Interviewer: All right, I'm a liar, but you're a bloated
plutocrat with pimples and B.O.

Mr. President: Let's make no mistake about this: we're talking
about legislation.

Interviewer: My dad's bigger than your dad.

Dan: I'm talking about the working class of this
country, and they're 100% behind me.

Interviewer: My dad's got a bigger stick than your dad.

Mr. President: That's a question which the country decided for
itself at the last election.

Interviewer:	Don't care.
Dan:	You should try working in the conditions that our members have to put up with.
Interviewer:	Softy.
Mr. President:	I've come up the hard way!
Interviewer:	Who's a softy?
Dan:	This government has lost touch with the grassroots.
Interviewer:	Ne neh-ni neh neh!
Mr. President:	It's a matter of priorities.
Interviewer:	Belt up.
Dan:	Priorities!
Interviewer:	Can't.
Mr. President:	There's a budget in a few weeks' time.
Interviewer:	You'd better.
Mr. President:	Look, I have called upon the cabinet as a matter of the utmost urgency to impress upon them the need for taking steps to improve the situation as it stands—taking into consideration the escalation of the inflation situation at this particular moment in time. We must seek, at the earliest opportunity, for some means of ensuring that change, when it comes (and believe me, it *will* come), is within the context of an ongoing maintenance of those standards of democratic integrity which have characterized all those involved in the struggle. It is time for abandoning so-called positions and taking a stand. Flexibility is the key word as we step into the foreseeable future to face the unforeseen. The time is coming—and I say this in all sincerity—when we do so not only at our peril.

Interviewer: He says . . . (*There is a long pause of total bafflement*) Er . . . uh . . . uh . . . (*These gradually turn into chimpanzee noises. The* INTERVIEWER *himself begins to turn into a chimpanzee as the lights fade . . .*)

Sharing the Joke

A MAN *is sitting on a bench reading a book. Another man* (TWO) *comes and joins him. He doesn't say anything for quite a long time. Then he speaks.*

Two: I meant to go on a camping trip last year. I hit on
         Michigan and New York as likely to provide
         some pleasing landscapes. *(Pause)* Unfortun-
         ately I forgot to rent the camper. *(Pause)* There's
         nothing that falls quite so flat as a camping trip
         without a camper. *(Pause)* Unless it's—huh
         huh!—unless it's a parachutist without a
         parachute. Huh huh! Yes.
         I've always been one to look for the humor in
         situations, you know. Life is full of humor if
         you just keep your eyes open for it. Huh huh!
         (Pause) But then you wouldn't see it so easily.
         Yes, humor! A good laugh is better than a tonic,
         isn't it? I can illustrate what I mean by recount-
         ing something that happened only yesterday. I
         had to go to see my dentist for my four-month-
         ly check-up. Not a lot of humor in *that*, you
         might think. Ah! Well—when I got in there I
         said to my dentist, "Is there anything wrong,
         Mr. Buy?" I call him Mr. Buy because his name
         is Purchase, you see. Huh! "Why do you ask?"
         says he. "Well I just thought," I said, "that you
         looked a bit down in the mouth." Huh huh!
         Yes. It's a funny thing, humor. Have you been
         in the park down the road? The new one by the
         river? Only I hear that, to save trouble, they've
         planted it with ready-vandalized trees! Huh

huh! *(Pause)* They haven't really. Yes, it's good
to have a laugh. I had quite a good laugh last
night at an insurance man's expense. He had
called to sell me some life insurance. I said,
"I'm afraid I don't need any; I'm an honest
man!" He fell for that one. "What do you mean
by that?" he asked me. "Well," I said, "don't
they say 'honesty is the best policy'?" My word,
that gave me and Mavis a chuckle!
We have a lot of laughs, Mavis and I. When we
were first married I used to put all sorts of
strange things down the bed to give her a
fright—hair curlers, wet sponges, light-bulbs;
and I used to amuse her no end by rolling up
bus-tickets and sticking them up my nose.
(Pause) They have those fare-boxes now, of
course. But there's still plenty of humor left in
life! I expect you noticed just now when I said,
"It's a funny thing, humor." That's just one example. There are plenty of others I could point
out for you; I've popped in quite a few jokes
during our little conversation.
      MAN *yawns loudly*
Well, I never! My wife's got a laugh *just* like
   yours . . . !

                    Blackout

Bibliography

He knew everything about literature except how to enjoy it.
Joseph Heller, *Catch 22*

*F*or a writer, everything he reads from Biggles to Bulgakov will contain lessons and smaller or larger inspirations. This list cannot, therefore, be exhaustive; it is bound to be personal to some extent, and a browse among the relevant sections in the local library will redress the balance. I have not, for instance, explored the glossier books which are being published these days on individual actors such as Olivier, Glenda Jackson, and Marlon Brando, but these can sometimes contain fascinating insights and scraps of advice and can often be picked up quite cheaply in second-hand bookshops.

There may be glaring omissions, but I have tried to list books which have the effect of opening the mind and the imagination as well as those which transmit facts and common sense, techniques, and practical advice.

General

Michael Billington, ed., *Performing Arts*. New York: Facts on File, 1980. On all aspects of performance including backstage. Lavishly illustrated.

P. Brook, *The Empty Space*. New York: Penguin, 1972. A fascinating, informed, and beautifully written introduction to the art of the theater.

Elizabeth Burns, *Theatricality*. London: Longman, 1972.

Edward Gordon Craig, *On the Art of the Theatre*. New York: Theatre Arts Books, 1980.

K. Elam, *The Semiotics of Theatre and Drama*. London: Methuen, 1980.

H. Gardner, *Religion and Literature*. London: Faber and Faber, 1971. A discussion of tragedy and poetry from a Christian perspective. Brilliant but academic.

J.L. Styan, *The Dark Comedy*. Cambridge University Press, 1962. How theater works; dissections and analyses; very readable, very wise.

———, *The Elements of Drama*. Cambridge University Press, 1960.

R. Williams, *Keywords*. New York: Oxford University Press, 1976. Theater and general culture.

Acting

C. Barker, *Theatre Games*. London: Methuen, 1977. Indispensable for teachers and organizers of workshops; great fun and induces mental and physical alertness.

R.L. Benedetti, *The Actor at Work*. Englewood Cliffs, NJ: Prentice-Hall, 1981.

Cicely Berry, *Voice and the Actor*. New York: Macmillan, 1974. Cicely Berry coaches the RSC.

M. Chekov, *To the Actor*. New York: Harper and Row, 1978.

J. Grotowski, *Towards a Poor Theatre*. London: Methuen, 1969. Interesting, extreme, much discussed.

Ronald Hayman, *Techniques of Acting*. London: Methuen, 1969.

Keith Johnstone, *Impro*. London: Faber and Faber, 1979. Excellent ideas and insights for actors.

Kristin Linklater, *Freeing the Natural Voice*. New York: Drama Book Specialists, 1976.

Litz Pisk, *The Actor and his Body*. New York: Theatre Arts Books, 1976.

Michael Redgrave, *The Actor's Ways and Means*. New York: Theatre Arts Books, 1979.

A. Scher and C. Verrall, *100+ Ideas for Drama*. London: Heinemann, 1975. Solid but unexciting.

Viola Spolin, *Improvisation for the Theatre*. Evanston, IL: Northwestern University Press, 1970.

Constantin Stanislavski, *An Actor Prepares*. New York: Theatre Arts Books, 1970.

Clive Swift, *The Job of Acting*. London: Harrap, 1976.

Directing

Edward Braun, *The Director and the Stage*. New York: Holmes & Meier, 1982.

Toby Cole and Helen Krich Chinoy, *Directors on Directing*. New York: Macmillan, 1976.

J. Fernald, *The Play Produced*. Deane, n.d.

———, *Sense of Direction*. Secker and Warburg, 1968. Very good advice to directors.

John Heilpern, *Conference of the Birds*. Penguin, 1979. Original and challenging.

Charles Marowitz, *The Act of Being*. New York: Taplinger Publishing Company, 1978. Idiosyncratic but thought-provoking.

Athene Seyler and Stephen Haggard, *The Craft of Comedy*. New York: Theatre Arts Books, 1957.

J.L. Stylan, *Modern Drama in Theory and Practice*. New York: Cambridge University Press, 1981. Intelligent and readable.

Stage Management

Hendrik Baker, *Stage Management and Theatrecraft*. New York: Theatre Arts Books, 1981.

Fredcrick Bentham, *The Art of Stage Lighting*. London: Pitman, 1976.

Richard Corson, *Stage Makeup*. Englewood Cliffs, NJ: Prentice-Hall, 1986.

Arnold S. and J. Michael Gillette, *Stage Scenery: Its Construction and Rigging*. New York: Harper and Row, 1981.

Jacquie Govier, *Create Your Own Stage Props*. Englewood Cliffs, NJ: Prentice-Hall, Inc., 1984.

Motley, *Designing and Making Stage Costumes*. New York: Watson-Guptill Publications, 1974. Motley is one of the great names of the theater. Wisdom plus experience.

Motley, *Theatre Props*. London: Studio Vista, 1975.

Richard Pilbrow, *Stage Lighting*. London: Studio Vista, 1970.

Francis Reid, *The Stage Lighting Handbook*. London: Adam & Charles Black, 1982. Everything you always wanted to know, etc.

C. Ray Smith, ed. *The Theatre Crafts of Make-Up, Masks and Wigs*. Toronto: Rodale Press, 1974.

David Welker, *Theatrical Set Design: The Basic Techniques*. Boston: Allyn and Bacon, 1979.

Administration

Francis Reid, *Theatre Administration*. London: Adam & Charles Black, 1983. Better be good because it is the only one I can find that looks even reasonable.

Writing

W.H. Auden, *The Enchafed Flood*. London, 1951, n.p.

N. Bagnall, *A Defence of Clichés*. London: Constable, 1985. How to be honest in English.

E.R. Bentley, *The Playwright as Thinker*. New York: Harcourt, Brace, Jovanovich, 1967.

P. Burbridge and M. Watts, *Time to Act*. London: Hodder and Stoughton, 1979.

————, *Lightning Sketches*. London: Hodder and Stoughton, 1981.

————, *Red Letter Days*. London: Hodder and Stoughton, 1986. All three contain very useful articles as well as material to perform.

C. Caudwell, *Illusion and Reality*. London, 1937, n.p.

H. Caudwell, *The Creative Impulse*. New York: Macmillan, 1953.

Joseph Chiari, *Realism and Imagination*. Barrie and Rockliff, 1960. Integrity v. Squalor.

Toby Cole, ed., *Playwrights on Playwriting*. New York: Hill and Wang, 1960.

D. Daiches, *A Study of Literature*. New York: Cornell University Press, 1948. What is it? Why is it?

T.S. Eliot, *The Sacred Wood*. London: Methuen, 1934. Not theater, but well worth reading.

U. Ellis-Fermor, *The Frontiers of Drama*. Methuen, n.d.

B. Gascoyne, *Twentieth Century Drama*. Hutchinson, 1962. Excellent introduction both to the big themes and the big names. Yes, that B. Gascoyne.

Robert Graves and Alan Hodge, *The Reader over Your Shoulder*. New York: Random House, 1979. A bit nit-picking, but a good corrective to modern sloppiness. Perhaps it should be balanced with . . .

Philip Howard, *The State of the Language*. Berkeley: University of California Press, 1980. Witty and sane.

Thomas Rice Henn, *The Harvest of Tragedy*. London: Methuen, 1956.

H. Jackson, *The Reading of Books*. London: Faber and Faber, 1946.

Walter Kerr, *How Not to Write a Play*. London, 1956, n.p.

H.D.F. Kitto, *Form and Meaning in Drama*. London, Methuen, 1964.

Arthur Koestler, *The Act of Creation*. London: Hutchinson, 1969. Not a practical book, but a fascinating glimpse into how the mind works. Not easy but rewarding.

C.S. Lewis, *An Experiment in Criticism*. Cambridge University Press, 1961. Short and very sweet.

————, *Study in Words*. Cambridge University Press, 1960.

————, *Of Other Worlds*. London: Bles, 1966.

J. Livingston Lowes, *The Road to Xanadu*. Boston: Houghton Mifflin, 1964. One of the most amazing books ever written. Traces the origins of a piece of literature in the reading, interests, and occupations of the writer. Almost answers that question, "How do you do it?"

L. Macneice, *Varieties of Parable*. Cambridge University Press, 1965. The difference between theme and subject; how meanings are made.

J. Mander, *The Writer and Commitment*. London, 1961, n.p.

C.E. Montague, *A Writer's Notes on His Trade*. Manchester, NH: Chatto and Windus, 1930. Literature and language discussed humbly and sensibly.

A. Nicoll, *The Theory of Drama*. London, 1931, n.p.

J. Sutherland, *English Satire*. Cambridge University Press, 1962. Definitions, forms, analysis; brief, deep, readable.

John V. Taylor, *The Go-Between God*. Oxford University Press, 1979. Looks slightly out of place here, but helped me to understand more about inspiration.

A.R. Thompson, *The Anatomy of Drama*. Berkeley: University of California, 1942.

A.R. Thompson, *The Dry Mock*. Berkeley: University of California, 1948. A study of irony.

G.W. Turner, *Stylistics*. New York: Penguin, 1973. How words make a difference.

Alan W. Watts, *Myth and Ritual in Christianity*. New York: Thames & Hudson, 1954.

Murray Watts, *Christianity and the Theatre*. Edinburgh: Handsel Press, 1986.